You know what the problem is about handling money God's way? It works. If you handle your money the way God tells you to in Scripture, you're going to build wealth. But if you don't have the spiritual and emotional backbone to carry that wealth, it will destroy your life. In *How to Be Rich*, Andy lays out clear principles for carrying that load, making sure your wealth remains a blessing not just for you, but for your family and community for generations to come.

Dave Ramsey, *New York Times* bestselling author
and nationally syndicated radio show host

My friend Andy has been teaching his churches this material for years. I am so grateful he has chosen to make it available to a broader audience. I know from my personal interaction with Sandra and Andy that this is not theory. This is how they live their lives and manage their personal finances. My hope is that the message of *How to Be Rich* will permeate our culture and spark a revival of Christ-centered generosity and stewardship.

John C. Maxwell, leadership author and speaker

When Andy originally presented this content to his churches, I asked for the outlines and repreached it to mine. When he told me he was publishing this content, I told him I would do everything I could to get it into as many hands as possible. That's how strongly I feel about this content. Buy it! Read it! Pass it on.

Craig Groeschel, pastor, LifeChurch.tv and author of
Fight and *The Christian Atheist*

How to Be Rich is liberating, fresh, convicting, and wise. It is a radical message in a friendly voice, and it c

John Ortberg, senior pastor of Menl
Church, and author of *Who Is*

Andy Stanley provides with *How to Be Rich* the most fundamental and fresh biblical approach to generosity, wealth, and stewardship. This is a revolution-starting, game-changing book. Our use of time, talent, and treasure is paramount to leading well and leaving a legacy. This message and book will change our churches, communities, and our culture for good. It's mandatory reading!

Brad Lomenick, author of *The Catalyst Leader*

Our culture bombards us with messages designed to make us feel deprived of more stuff, while half the world lives on less than two dollars a day. Andy makes a fresh, compelling case that the first step to following Jesus' call to be wise and generous stewards is to recognize that we are already rich. Only then will we discover the joy and freedom of putting our trust in God and not our bank accounts.

Jonathan Reckford, CEO,
Habitat for Humanity International

In a culture that sees money as the way to happiness, Andy Stanley explains that the real value of money is that it provides the opportunity for us to make a difference beyond ourselves. Reading *How to Be Rich* will unlock the message of why God so richly provides for us, and will teach you not to trust in riches but in him who richly provides.

Mike Kendrick, CEO, iDisciple —
A Family Christian Company

An old hymn says, "Jesus is all the world to me ... my life, my joy, my all." If you can't touch that reality deeply but want to, read this book. Careful though; it might change you and your world for good in ways you never imagined.

Jimmy Mellado, president and CEO,
Compassion International

ANDY STANLEY

❖

HOW TO
BE RICH

IT'S NOT WHAT YOU HAVE.
IT'S WHAT YOU DO
WITH WHAT YOU HAVE.

ZONDERVAN

How to Be Rich
Copyright © 2013 by Andy Stanley

This title is also available as a Zondervan ebook. Visit www.zondervan.com/ebooks.

This title is also available in a Zondervan audio edition. Visit www.zondervan.fm.

Requests for information should be addressed to:

Zondervan, *Grand Rapids, Michigan 49530*

ISBN 978-0-310-49487-4

Cover design: Michelle Lenger
Interior design: David Conn

Printed in the United States of America

13 14 15 16 17 18 /DCI/ 21 20 19 18 17 16 15 14 13 12 11 10 9 8 7 6 5 4 3 2 1

For Howard Bowen.
You certainly know how.

CONTENTS

ACKNOWLEDGMENTS

No book is the product of individual effort. This book is certainly no exception. *How to Be Rich* reflects the insight, creativity, editing, and writing skills of a talented team of people that I'm privileged to call friends. To begin, I would like to thank Craig Groeschel for encouraging me to put this content in book form. Honestly, I'm not sure it would have happened if he hadn't finally threatened to publish these ideas under his name. Thanks, Craig!

On the creative and content side of the equation, my longtime friend Ben Ortlip deserves far more credit than a sentence or two can provide. His illustrations and insights made this book so much better and so much more accessible than I could have ever done on my own. Thank you, Ben!

On the production side, this project would have never gotten to the finish line without the indefatigable labor of Suzy Gray. Once again, when I wanted to be *done*, Suzy wanted it to be *better*. Suzy, thank you for your attention to detail. Thank you for reading and rereading and rereading again.

To John Raymond at Zondervan, thank you for the enthusiasm you expressed early on for the content of this book. Thank you for leveraging your influence to help us get this message into the hearts of believers around the world.

Books always reflect something of the life journeys of their authors. This book is certainly no exception. Generosity has always been easy for me. Primarily because of the way I was raised. Being generous as a family has been even easier because of who I married. Anytime I've suggested we do something crazy in the realm of generosity, Sandra smiles and says, "That's what I love about you." And that's what I love about her.

INTRODUCTION

Like most young men, I grew up hoping to be R-I-C-H. Not filthy rich. Not private-jet rich. Just rich enough to be able to do what I wanted when I wanted, without worrying about how much it cost. You know, average rich. My initial strategy for attaining *rich* was to be a rock star and "live in hilltop houses drivin' fifteen cars."[1] So I taught myself to play the guitar and piano, rounded up a few high school friends, and started a band. I had no doubt that I was on my way to fortune and fame. Actually, I really didn't care about the fame part. From the beginning I've been convinced that it is better to be rich than famous. Anonymity was a price I was willing to pay.

Now, as you might imagine, my parents weren't thrilled with my career choice. My dad in particular. When people

---

1. Nickelback, "Rockstar" lyrics.

asked me what I was planning to do when I grew up, my dad would give me that look and then answer for me, "Andy hasn't decided yet."

Needless to say, the rock star thing didn't work out. If country music had been as big in the '70s as it is now, I might have had a chance. And honestly, "Sometimes when I play that old six-string, I think about you, wonder what went wrong."[2]

Let's move on.

Once I accepted the fact that I didn't have the chops for the music biz, I was forced to come up with another get-rich career scheme. And that's when it hit me—the ministry! I'll be a pastor! After all, pastors have lots of money.

Now, while that may be true to a limited extent today, back then I had never heard of a rich preacher. As you probably know, my dad is a pastor. My parents never owned their own home until I was in middle school. Before that we lived in a parsonage, a house that a church purchased for the pastor and his family to use. It "came with the job," was just part of the package. Kind of like being the President of the United States. Except we had to mow the lawn. And unlike the first family, we had to get permission to redecorate or repaint or re-anything. After all, it wasn't our house. It was "the people's house." As in church people. And church people can be particular about what you do with their house. And that's understandable. In those days, pastors didn't stay more than three or four years. So there was no point in making a lot of expensive changes for someone who wasn't going to be around that long.

---

2. Bryan Adams, "Summer of '69" lyrics.

All that to say, the notion of getting rich by way of pastoring never dawned on me. As I said, I'd never met a rich preacher. And we certainly weren't rich. Not the kind of rich I was dreaming of anyway. We always had enough. But rich is about having *more* than enough. We had what we needed. But rich is about having more than you need. Rich is about having extra. Isn't it?

When I was in fifth grade, we lived in a small town in Florida where my dad was the pastor of the First Baptist Church. The parsonage was located in a typical small-town, middle-class neighborhood. Not upper middle class. Just middle class. One afternoon, my dad asked me to ride with him when we took our housekeeper home. Yes, we had a housekeeper. Back then we referred to her as our maid. And she was fine with that. Actually, she was proud of that. She was the preacher's maid, and she made sure all her maid friends knew about it. Normally she drove. But on this particular afternoon her car was in the shop, so we drove her home.

Turns out, I had never been to that particular part of our small town. The houses were small, the yards were mostly dirt, and there was junk everywhere. I still remember feeling uncomfortable. When we got to her house, she invited us in. I remember thinking, *I don't want to go in there.* For whatever reason, we didn't. When we got back home, our house looked large by comparison. Our yard looked manicured by comparison. Even our car felt fine in comparison to what I saw in our maid's neighborhood.

It was while we were living in that same house that a friend from church came over to play. His name was Bruce.

I can still remember Bruce standing in our kitchen, looking around, and saying, "Andy, your house is so big. Are you rich?" I was so uncomfortable. Rich? We weren't rich. And our house wasn't big. Our house was normal size. But when we took Bruce home that evening, I understood. By comparison, our house was big. By comparison, I'm sure it looked to Bruce as if we were rich. Heck, by comparison, we *were* rich.

And therein lies the problem, doesn't it?

Rich is the other guy. Rich is that other family. Rich isn't just having extra. Rich is having as much extra as the person who has more extra than you do. Rich is having more than you currently have. If that's the case, you can be rich and not *know* it. You can be rich and not *feel* it. You can be rich and not act like it. And that is a problem. In fact, that's why I wrote this book.

If you purchased this book with your own money, or could have had you been so inclined, you are much further ahead of the financial game than you might imagine. And if that's hard for you to imagine, no worries. For the next seven chapters, I'm going to do my best to convince you that you are in fact a *have* rather than a *have-not*. Better yet, I'm going to use everything in my arsenal of persuasive powers to convince you that you are rich. Once you're convinced, I'm going to walk you through a short passage from the New Testament that instructs us rich people how to be good at it. Because, as you are about to discover, assuming you haven't observed this already, most rich people aren't all that good at being rich. Perhaps, you included.

While this is a new publication for me, this is not a new message. Every fall for the past seven years, I've stood in front of our Atlanta-area churches and told 'em they are a bunch of *haves* who act like *have-nots* and that God and I aren't happy about it! Okay, that's not exactly how I phrased it. But when it comes to this particular topic, I've been known to be uncomfortably bold.

Our churches' journey began with a message series I preached in 2007 entitled *How to Be Rich*. Two things prompted the series. First, our culture's incessant messages about how to get rich when, in fact, most of us got rich a long time ago and nobody told us. Second, Paul's instructions to Timothy regarding how rich Christians are to behave. After studying the passage, I was left with the realization that a lot of rich Christians are not very good at being rich. Then it dawned on me: Well of course they're not. Nobody has taught them how! So for four weekends I navigated our congregation through the terms and conditions of Paul's instructions to rich people.

The series resulted in a lot of healthy conversations. So I followed up the next year with a message on the same topic combined with a month-long generosity campaign aimed at our local communities. I told our congregants that we were going to practice being rich so we would be good at it should we ever be so fortunate. The generosity campaign included a hefty donation goal that was due by the end of the week. Most of it came in that day. In addition to financial support for local and international charities, we asked them to donate two or three hours of their time over the course of the month by volunteering at the charities chosen to receive the funds we collected. And by the way, none of these charities asked us for money. That's what makes a *Be Rich* campaign so much fun.

Behind the scenes, a team of church staff and volunteers went into our local communities to find charities that were making a measurable difference but who could use a little wind in their sails. So imagine their surprise a few weeks later when a handful of our folks showed up at their doors with checks. In most cases, big checks. Checks they were not expecting. And imagine the reaction a few weeks after that when we opened our services with a video of staff and volunteers at these world-class charities receiving their surprise donations. Not a dry eye in the place. Suddenly and simultaneously, everybody in the house experienced the truth of Jesus' words that it is, in fact, more blessed to give than to receive.

In the fall of 2012, I challenged our churches to give $1.5 million toward our *Be Rich* giving initiative. They gave $5.2 million. In a week. And we in turn gave 100 percent of it away. No shipping and handling costs. No overhead or operating expenses. No expensive vacations for the pastor and his family. We gave it all away. In addition, our congregants provided 34,000 volunteer hours to local charities that are volunteer dependent. And if that weren't enough, we collected 20,332 Operation Christmas Child shoeboxes for Samaritan's Purse—the largest collection they've ever received from a local church. Pretty good for rich rehearsal.

Am I bragging? Heck, yeah. I'm so proud of our churches

that I get misty-eyed just thinking about the difference they made and continue to make. Two months ago my daughter, Allie, and I visited our international partner in San Salvador, La Casa de Mi Padre (My Father's House), a group home for children who can't live with their families for a variety of heartbreaking reasons. Gary Powell, executive director, picked us up at the airport and asked, "How do you like my truck?" Before I could answer, he smiled and said, "It's a *Be Rich* truck. Thank you." While we were there, we spent time with a local construction crew building a large retaining wall on the edge of their property. As we were leaving, Gary leaned over and said, "That's a *Be Rich* wall. Tell your folks 'Thanks.'" While visiting the children's home, Gary introduced me to their newest employee, a licensed marriage and family counselor, a position they desperately needed as they seek to reconnect children with their families. As we left her office, Gary smiled and said, "Thanks to *Be Rich*. Thank you."

Now, I realize you and your church are already doing amazing things in your community and around the world. I assume you have your own stories you could tell. My purpose in writing this book is not to replace or improve anything you are currently doing. My goal is to create a tool that will force conversation and reflection around the topic of what to do with what we have. On this point Jesus could not have been clearer. It's not what you have that matters. It's what you *do* with what you have that will count either for you or against you in the kingdom of heaven.

Just so we're clear, I'm not a philanthropist. While I care

about the poor, the issue of local or global poverty doesn't keep me up at night. I'm concerned for the plight of children. But I'm not on a mission to get all the available orphans in the world adopted into Christian homes. Though, like you, I sure wish they could be. My passion, and a major reason I want to get this message into your hands, is my concern for the reputation and cultural positioning of the local church. I want you to help me reanchor the church to undeniable, mind-boggling, culture-shifting demonstrations of compassion and generosity. Because, as we will discuss in chapter 7, generosity was the hallmark of the early church. They did for those who could not do or would not do anything in return. That was new. That got people's attention. Eventually, it shifted and shaped the moral conscience of the West.

But for that to happen, there must be several shifts in our thinking. And one of those shifts relates to how we define *rich*.

So here we go . . .

Chapter 1

CELEBRATION IS IN ORDER

You can never be too rich or too thin.

Wallis Simpson, Duchess of Windsor

By the time they brought the patient to him, the situation looked grave. "Miss A," as she was called in medical journals, was visibly stricken, and her motor skills had been reduced to semi-controlled trembles—the telltale movements of someone nearing the end. In the confusing mix of symptoms, her family suspected tuberculosis or a blood disease. She looked less like a treatable patient and more like a discarded cadaver from behind the town hospice. Her cheeks were sunken and her skin was like cheesecloth draped over a fossil. The notion that this doctor could save her was a long shot. The possibility that she would make a complete recovery was inconceivable.

Miss A's pulse was an exceptionally low forty-six, and her respiration was weak. But there was a nervous energy about her that suggested very high hormone levels. It didn't make sense. Her organ function, urine, and appetite were all normal. And yet she was clearly dying.

In 1866, modern medicine wasn't even a dream yet. There were no CAT scans or MRIs or tests to determine blood counts or endocrine levels. The practice of medicine was little more than a catalog of barbaric experiments. Common techniques included bloodletting, opium injections, electric shock, and turpentine enemas. These grotesque procedures were often the final nail in the coffin for someone already weakened by fever or infection. Diseases were the leading cause of death, followed closely by the trial methods devised to treat them.

But Miss A had been brought to Sir William Gull. And he wasn't like other doctors of his era. He valued observation over action. He was slow to treat and quick to care. While he was credited with numerous medical breakthroughs, his greatest skill was his keen bedside manner.

Perhaps it was his experience with the epidemics of the day—cholera, typhoid, and smallpox—that taught Gull to look beyond symptoms for the deeper cause of a disease. He was a holistic problem solver. And the baffling case of Miss A would require nothing less.

Most physicians would have surrendered her to death or turned her into a human lab specimen, possibly cauterizing her spine to stimulate healing or injecting her with creative concoctions designed to kill everything but the patient. But Gull was not intoxicated by the reckless practices of the day. "We treat people, not diseases," he would remind his students. He believed that many cases would resolve themselves if the physicians didn't meddle too much. Once when a lady with a rare skin disease was brought to him, Gull simply placed an extraction from one of her sores under a microscope, showed it to her, and reassured her that she would recover. It was the only treatment he gave her. And it worked.

Gull did not consider it a sign of incompetence to admit he lacked the answer to a problem either. "Fools and savages explain; wise men investigate," was one of his favorite sayings. So whenever he wasn't sure, he resorted to basic nursing duties while he continued to observe. He once wrote, "Acquaint yourself with the causes that have led up to the disease. Don't guess at them, but know them through and through if you can; and if you do not know them, know that you do not, and still inquire."

Only by immersing himself in the patient's experience did Gull manage to discover what others overlooked. The case of Miss A was to be a perfect example of this dedication. For two years he oversaw her care, methodically nursing her back to full health with a regimen of remedies. Little by little, her strength returned. And little by little, Gull gathered the certainty he needed to declare a name for the disease that had almost taken Miss A's life.

After careful consideration, he dubbed it: *anorexia nervosa*.

That's right. Anorexia. Sir William Gull had discovered one of the most puzzling diseases of the twentieth century—more than a hundred years before its time. He gave it the name that still haunts headlines today. And all on his own, he successfully treated dozens of cases—Miss B, Miss C, and so on—reversing the devastation and returning them to normal life. Gull meticulously documented the details of each one. And with each one he deepened our understanding of this crippling disease that offered virtually no clinical factors that a medical staff could treat.

Anorexia was one of the first psychological diseases spawned by modern industrialized culture, and it has become one of its most enduring. "It is remarkable," wrote one of Gull's colleagues, "that a disease which no one had recognized before its existence and characters were established by Gull, has since been found to exist not only in this country and on the Continent, but in America and Australia."

Anorexia is among a class of diseases that attacks the body despite the fact that it exists only in the hidden recesses of the brain—an invisible invader wreaking all-too-visible havoc. It's not a foreign agent like a virus or a bacteria or a cancerous cell. It is a sinister deception that hijacks the mind and programs it to destroy its own host organism.

RECIPE FOR DELUSION

Gull's remarkable diagnosis makes perfect sense looking backward. Anorexia was an irrational delusion of the mind— a by-product of the social pressures of the day. Throughout the 1800s, civilizations were slowly shifting away from their agrarian foundations. Cities were growing bigger and bigger. Cultures were being consolidated as people shared the same buildings and read the same newspapers. Social norms were established on a scale never seen before. Lifestyle magazines began to blanket communities, propagating unwritten codes of conduct and rules for conformity. By 1850, the number of British periodicals shot to over 100,000, and the use of engravings made pictures and sketches a regular part of the literary experience. For the first time in history, it was possible to take any idea and promote it on a massive, graphic scale. The age of the mega-peddler had begun.

Thanks to industrialization, everything was bigger too.

Basic goods became enormous industries. News sources became mass media. Large factories churned out products. The age of needs-based marketing was gone. To move the massive supply of goods being manufactured, industries needed to manufacture an equally massive level of demand. And one of the concepts they began to promote was the ideal body image. Corsets were in style. Fashion was imperative. And the importance of having an hourglass figure was emphasized for women everywhere.

Whenever something is blown out of proportion in culture, it has a ripple effect. Other things get blown out of proportion too.

The ideal body in the 1800s was anything but thin. It was plump and shapely. But the corset took things in a whole new direction. To accentuate the full-figured look that everyone wanted, the lace-up corset was designed to shrink the waist, giving the appearance of fullness everywhere else. It was mostly an optical illusion at first. But the custom evolved into a trend that brought some very real ramifications. To keep up with the Joneses, women began drawing their corsets tighter and tighter. Then Mrs. Jones would tighten hers again. Over time, a woman could push things around and train her midsection to achieve enormous reductions in her waist. At its peak, the standard for an "attractive" waist was anything under twenty inches. It was not uncommon for a woman's waist to be sixteen to eighteen inches after months of training. Many women learned to breathe using only the top portion of their lungs, which caused mucus to fill their lower lungs and left them with persistent coughs.

The health implications of corsets were debated rigorously. It was a hot topic in the same way that gun control or the deficit is argued about today. It even had a name: "the corset controversy." The newspapers were filled with editorials arguing both sides. The volume of op-ed submissions on this topic hit its highest point in 1860 — about the time Miss A began to struggle. While opponents called the corset a form of oppression, many of the staunchest supporters were the women who wore them. "There is not a single fashionable woman who does not wear a corset," one woman wrote. Another said, "Go without my stays? Never. I wouldn't do anything so untidy. I think a woman without corsets is most unsightly. You cannot look smart and have a pretty figure without stays. It is impossible."[3]

In the middle of this social discourse, the young Miss A was developing her worldview and learning the ways of the world — exploring the meaning of life and discovering how to fit in. Undoubtedly, she would have been pondering these things at the height of the corset controversy.

Under the weight of this social pressure, Miss A considered the implications of being fashionable versus being comfortable. And perhaps, like numerous others, she concluded that the risk of not measuring up to society's definition of beauty was too great.

A common myth about anorexics holds that when they look in the mirror, they see a fat person. That's not really accurate. What they see is someone who would be better off

3. See *A Collection of the Public Writings of William Withey Gull, Vol. 2*, edited and arranged by T. D. Acland (London: New Sydenham Society, 1896); digitized by Princeton University, Nov. 24, 2008.

just a little bit thinner. For Miss A, it probably meant she needed to tighten up her corset another inch or more, a goal she obviously accomplished several times over as she returned to her mirror and got the same feedback each time. A thin waist is an abstract ideal. It's difficult to define and impossible to own outright. At some point for Miss A, it became an irrational, immeasurable, and unattainable pursuit.

There's something about living in a civilized, industrialized culture that compromises rational thought. Agrarian people didn't seem to wrestle with it as much. It's easier to keep your priorities in perspective when they revolve around the tangible elements of survival—like your next meal. The richer you get, however, the more your priorities begin to separate from actual needs. When all of our basic requirements are met, our appetites for progress don't turn off. We simply turn from the things we *need* to the things we *want*. And that's when we enter the world of the subjective. *Wants* are harder to define. And easier to confuse.

In America today, there are more than eight million cases of anorexia. And it's no secret that our culture's emphasis on body image plays a huge role in that. We live in a culture that encourages us to be thin. At a time when we enjoy the most abundant food supply in the history of the world, the number of people voluntarily starving themselves to death continues to rise. The human mind is a powerful, yet fragile thing.

The irony for anorexics is that they've already mastered the thing they're working so hard to achieve. They're really good at losing weight. But they're really bad at knowing when to stop. For them, the destination has taken a backseat to the journey. They're so absorbed in the effort to *get* thin, they no longer recognize when they *are* thin.

THE RICHEST PEOPLE IN HISTORY

Anorexics aren't the only ones adrift in the world of the subjective. Our civilized, industrialized culture invites the rest of us to compromise rational thought in another way. Not only does it encourage us to be thin, it also encourages us to be rich. And the richer we become as a nation, the more our priorities seem to separate from what are true needs. Our basic requirements have long since been met, but our appetites for progress haven't begun to turn off. When we look in the mirror, we see altered versions of what's really there.

We're so absorbed in the effort to *get* rich, we no longer recognize when we *are* rich.

The truth is we're already rich. No matter where you stand on the economy, we live in the richest time of the richest nation in history. In fact, if you can read this, you're automatically rich by global standards. And it's not just because you can read and have access to books, but because you've been given the individual freedom to do so, not to mention the time. That's not the case everywhere. And it certainly hasn't been the case throughout history.

If you can read this, you're automatically rich by global standards.

For example, in our Western culture today, we observe a five-day workweek. Think about what that means. Most people have to work only five days in order to have seven days' worth of food and shelter and clothing and health care. We take it for granted. But that's unique to our little window in history. And it's still not the case everywhere. What's more, there are households of three, four, or more people that send only one person out into the workplace to earn money. And with that one person's earnings, the entire family can amass enough money in five days to give them food and shelter for seven days. In many cultures, that's inconceivable. Outside of work, that leaves at least fifty hours per week for nothing but leisure. Most people in the world can only imagine such luxuries.

But let's be honest. Those examples don't really prove you're rich. They only serve to convince you that you're not poor. My hunch is you're a lot richer than you realize. It just doesn't feel like it. So let me give you a few more scenarios to consider.

If I told you I was offering you a job with a salary of $37,000 a year, would you feel rich? Probably not. Chances are, you wouldn't even be interested. A salary of $37,000 would represent a pay cut for most Americans. But for 96 percent of the world's population, $37,000 a year would be a significant increase.

Maybe there was a time when that sounded like a lot of money to you. And it should. In fact, if you earn more than $37,000 a year, you are in the top 4 percent of wage earners in the world! Congratulations! You are in the 4 percent club. You are rich! Yet I'm guessing this startling realization didn't cause you to leave the comfort of your couch to dance around the room. But you should have. On the world's scale, you should have no problems at all, other than a handful of rich-person problems. Problems that the majority of folks on this planet would love to have. Bad cell phone coverage? That's a rich-people problem. Can't decide where to go on vacation? Rich-people problem. Computer crashed? Slow Internet? Car trouble? Flight delays? Amazon doesn't have your size? All rich-people problems. Next time there's a watering ban in your neighborhood, just remember that many people, mostly women, carry jugs on their heads for hundreds of yards just so they can have water for cooking and drinking. They can't imagine a place where there's so much extra water that house after house just sprays it all over the ground.

Feeling guilty? I hope not. That's not my purpose. On the contrary, I'm hoping our time together leaves you feeling grateful. Guilt rarely results in positive behavior. But gratitude? Great things flow from a heart of gratitude. More on that later.

While we are comparing, consider this. What we call "poverty" today would have been considered middle class just a few generations ago. In 2000, the average "poor" family had goods and services rivaling middle-class families of the 1970s: 60 percent had microwaves, 50 percent had air conditioners, 93 percent had color televisions, and 60 percent had video recorders. More impressive is the income mobility within our economy. Most poor families don't stay poor. Over the sixteen-year period tracked by one study, 95 percent of the families in the lowest income quintile climbed the economic ladder to higher quintiles. Over 80 percent moved to the top three quintiles, qualifying them as middle class or better. As Michael Cox, an economist with the Federal Reserve, noted, "The rich may have gotten a little richer, but the poor have gotten much richer."

Gallup conducted a poll to see how different socioeconomic groups defined "rich." Not surprisingly, everybody had a different definition—and nobody thought he fit it. For each and every person, "rich" was roughly double the amount possessed by the person defining it. In other words, when they interviewed people who earned $30,000 a year, that group defined "rich" as someone who earns $60,000. When they interviewed people who earned $50,000 a year, the magic number was $100,000.

Similarly, *Money* magazine asked its readers how much money it would take to make them feel rich. And according to the average reader of *Money* magazine, a person would need $5 million in liquid assets to be considered rich. Based on the trend found in the Gallup poll, the readers of *Money* magazine probably averaged about $2.5 million in net worth (half their definition of "rich"). Therefore, if we asked people worth $5 million to define "rich," they would probably say it was anyone worth $10 million. And on and on it goes.

The moral of the story? "Rich" is a moving target. No matter how much money we have or make, we will probably never consider ourselves rich. The biggest challenge facing rich people is that they've lost their ability to recognize that they're rich.

> "Rich" is a moving target. No matter how much money we have or make, we will probably never consider ourselves rich.

Silly rich people.

Hang on; our housekeeper just told me that our yard people tracked mud across our pool deck.

A THEORY OF RELATIVITY

We suffer from Maslow's dilemma. Surely you remember Abraham Maslow and his "hierarchy of needs"? No? Maslow used a pyramid to explain a phenomenon we've all experienced. In essence, he said our needs are always changing depending on our circumstances. His model starts at the bottom with what we'd all agree are basic needs, and it progresses all the way up to things that amount to luxuries—at least for the people who haven't acquired them yet.

So here's the dilemma. As Maslow's model suggests, no matter where we are on the pyramid, we always want something *more*. When you're hungry and thirsty, *more* is simply food and water. That's certainly understandable. But once you graduate to being fed and hydrated, *more* becomes basic safety and security. That's reasonable too. Once you're convinced the borders are safe and there's peace in the land, *more* shifts again and your emotional needs become the focus—things like love, acceptance, and a sense of belonging—things that hadn't occurred to you when you were hungry. Once we possess all of those things, we'll find ourselves longing for achievement, a sense of purpose, and self-actualization—*more*. By instinct, we tend to be oriented in the direction of progress.

And there's no rest from this perpetual drive.

We find ourselves wanting *more* within each of Maslow's stages too. Even when a food source is found, it's just a matter of time before people look for ways to improve it. No matter how good we've got it, we always manage to entertain the idea that we might be able to do a little better. If you've ever shopped for a car, or sold a house, or traded stocks, or chosen a date for the prom, you can relate.

No matter where you are in your Maslovian journey, the tendency is to think more about what's in front of you and less about what's behind you. It's human nature. As long as you're heading *up* the pyramid, your focus will be on what you *don't* have. And you're less aware of what you *do* have. Only when life turns us in the other direction do we look back and notice how good we had it all along.

RAGS AND RICHES

As I mentioned in the introduction, my purpose in writing this book is to help rich Jesus followers get better at being rich. Even if you're not convinced you're rich, you probably hope to be. And should you ever admit that you have, in fact, crossed that imaginary line, I want you to be good at it. After all, most rich people aren't. For starters, they're not very good at staying rich. And somehow that always surprises us. We assume that rich people are smart people. Otherwise they wouldn't be so rich, right? So when we meet people who are richer than us, we often conclude that they're smarter than us too. When they join the conversation, we listen more carefully. We give extra weight to their opinions. And when it comes to making decisions, their perspectives get special consideration. But richer doesn't mean smarter.

When people get rich suddenly, they're almost never good at it. Maybe it's the lack of practice. A lot of professional athletes get rich suddenly, and they're often terrible at it. According to *Sports Illustrated*, an amazing 78 percent of NFL players find themselves bankrupt or financially stressed within two years of retirement. And 60 percent of NBA players are broke within five years of walking off the court.

How could that be? We mere mortals think to ourselves, *If I were in their place, I would never let that happen.* And it's not just athletes. One study of lottery winners showed that nearly half had spent their entire winnings within five years. Five years! While some rich people are bad at keeping their money, just about all of them are bad at being generous with it. Studies show that the richer people get, the smaller the percentage of money they give away. People in the median income bracket in the United States (around $50,000) give about 6 percent of their income to charities. That's not too bad. Now, if median earners can manage to be that generous, doesn't it make sense that wealthier people would give away an even greater percentage? That's not the case. When you look at earners in the $200,000 bracket, the level of giving drops to 4 percent. Instead of giving more, they give less. And the higher you go, the lower the percentage. Just one more bit of evidence that most rich people aren't very good at being rich. As you know, there's a plethora of books that teach people how to *get* rich. But statistically, that's not our problem. On a global scale, we're already rich. What we need are instructions on how to *be* rich now that so many of us are there. Instructions that a handful of rich people seem to have figured out on their own.

The richer people get, the smaller the percentage of money they give away.

I bet you've met some rich people who were good at being rich. They were generous. They knew how to take care of money without losing it. They weren't overcome by delusional thinking. Instead, they seemed to possess qualities that money can't buy. In fact, while they possessed a lot of money, it was evident that their money didn't possess them. And you found that refreshing, didn't you?

So how do they do it? I'll give you a hint: Being good at being rich begins with embracing a reality very few people are comfortable embracing. And just like Miss A, who was unable to see and embrace the truth that she was already thin, when we avoid what's true, we get ourselves into trouble. People who are good at being rich are the ones who are willing to admit they are, in fact, rich. Until you relax into the reality that you *are* rich, you will never become intentional about getting good at it. Instead you will spend the lion's share of your time and energy trying to cross a finish line that you probably crossed tens of thousands of dollars ago.

But hey, no pressure. This is just the first chapter. Besides, you are not alone. While we all wrestle with the difference between *becoming* rich and *being* rich, some wrestle with it more than others.

Chapter 2

LEARNING CURVE

*Wealth is like sea-water; the more we
drink, the thirstier we become.*

Arthur Schopenhauer

Being good at being rich is an acquired skill. It requires learning. Practice. Discipline. Like children, wealth doesn't come with a set of instructions. Having lots of money doesn't make you good at being rich any more than having lots of children makes you good at parenting. They are mutually exclusive. Think about it this way. If you took our nation's thirst for but lack of definition of wealth and applied it to children, everybody would be trying to give birth to as many sons and daughters as possible with little or no thought of how to raise them. We've all seen parents like that. It's not a good strategy for raising children, and it's not a good strategy for being rich.

Nowhere is the gap between *being rich* and *being good at it* more evident than with inherited wealth. Our country is home to a growing subculture of obscenely wealthy families. Talk about living in the richest time in history; data from the Federal Reserve shows that in 2000, the number of families worth $100 million or more was 7,000. Today that number is closer to 20,000. Families worth $10 million or more — charmingly referred to as "junior wealth" by financial planners — now number close to a million. The richest 1 percent of the U.S. population earns more than the national income of France or Italy. Think about that. And every year, thousands of these blue bloods pass on their estates to the next generations ... heirs who played no part in earning them ... heirs whose only qualifications are their last names! It's the financial equivalent of being strapped into an Indy racing car for your first driving lesson—during the race.

Within this special class of people, the amount of money that passes from one generation to the next just keeps on growing. Boston College's Center on Wealth and Philanthropy reported that inheritances during a five-year period ending in 2007 were 50 percent larger than the previous five years. Fifty percent. The issues surrounding this phenomenon are so significant, they've spawned an entire industry of subject-matter experts who deal with generational wealth. Firms with names like Wealthbridge Partners, Family Wealth Alliance, and Relative Solutions have become the gathering spots for parents whose greatest fear is that their child will be the next out-of-control heiress to star in a viral video on YouTube. These firms call their collective challenge "Rich Kid Syndrome."

And I know what you are thinking right now: *I would love to have that problem.* Hang on; we'll come back to that in a page or two.

Since the time of the earliest aristocrats, super-rich families have struggled with how to prepare their children for immense wealth. And who can blame them? Imagine having an estate worth $100 million or more. There are all kinds of different assets parked in a variety of investments. The economy is constantly shifting. Old technologies become obsolete. Today's hottest craze is tomorrow's dinosaur. And staple commodities, including real estate, fluctuate in value too. If you're not careful, you can lose 10 or 20 million dollars in a single month. Put together a few bad years and you could lose everything, or even end up owing money. It happens all the time. So you spend most of your adult life learning the art of managing your estate in a way that at least maintains it, if not grows it steadily. It's really not as easy as it looks. Just ask Lord Grantham of *Downton Abbey.*

Then one day you look in the mirror and see an older version of yourself looking back. You've done a good job with your estate, and you have a deep appreciation for how much effort it takes to preserve it, not to mention adding to it. Suddenly it occurs to you that your money is about to outlive you. At some point you'll need to hand over management to another capable person. And the leading candidate is the kid in the nursery at the end of the hall. So like countless wealthy parents before you, you awkwardly begin the process of preparing your child for the job. Why? Because you know that *simply possessing wealth doesn't make you good at managing it.* They are two entirely different things.

Simply possessing wealth doesn't make you good at managing it.

One of the biggest complicating factors is that wealthy people don't like to talk about money. At all. It's an unwritten rule of the *über*-rich. Discussing money is considered self-demeaning, even vulgar. I'll explain why in a moment.

But ask anyone on the list of the richest people in the world to talk about his money and he'll probably decline the interview. This is especially true when someone's wealth was inherited. Pharmaceutical heir Andrew Solomon explains, "Talking about money causes people not to take you seriously when talking about other things." It's as if acknowledging that your money is a big deal somehow makes you less of a big deal, like a stand-in for your own life. The tail not only wags the dog, but it chases it too.

Money is important to rich people. But rich people don't want their money to be the most important thing about them. And when you're worth hundreds of millions, that's an enormous challenge. About the only thing you can do is pretend it doesn't exist — at least verbally. As a result, the natural tendency is to avoid the subject with everyone, including family members. That's why they don't like talking about it. Obviously, this only widens the gap between money and the instructions for how to handle it. So the people who need to have conversations about money the most are often the least likely to have them.

For all these reasons, *being rich* is not the same as *being good at it.*

But hold on.

Don't go thinking this doesn't apply to you.

You may not have $100 million in your family, but that doesn't mean you're any different. Remember, on a global scale, you're rich too. And chances are, you're not any better at being rich. Whether you're in the richest 1 percent of the world, or if you're only in the richest 4 percent, you're in an elite class on the world stage. And just like your *über*-rich peers, it's no guarantee that you've ever learned how to be good at it.

Financially speaking, the difference between you and Bill Gates is smaller than the difference between you and the average person living outside the U.S. To most people, your bank accounts look virtually the same. In fact, years ago Bill Gates traveled to India on a philanthropic visit. In a neighborhood outside a large city, he spent time conversing with an Indian woman in her hut. Through a translator, they discussed the state of health care and other needs her people faced. After he left, a journalist asked the woman if she realized that the richest man in the world had just been in her house. Unfazed, she remarked that everybody who visits from the West is rich. In her eyes, the average American is so rich, she views them all the same.

POSSESSING WEALTH AND VICE VERSA

I've never been invited to join any of the firms I mentioned above—the ones that help families navigate those harrowing obstacles of dealing with $100 million or more. So I don't know what they teach their members. But it's nice to know they exist should I ever need their services one day.

What I do know, however, is that we're not much different from them. We may not think of ourselves as wealthy, but we suffer from our own little versions of Rich Kid Syndrome. We're not any better at being moderately rich than our millionaire neighbors are at being *über*-rich. We need to acquire the management skills that match our level of wealth in the world.

Assuming that you are starting to get comfortable with the fact that you *are rich*, the next step is to acknowledge an invisible dynamic that affects every rich person. Being good at being rich is not just a matter of deciding what to do with your money. You must also concern yourself with what your money is doing with you—or, more accurately, *to* you. This should be the starting point for any education on how to *be* rich. Money has an effect on its owners. And that effect, in turn, alters the way they see and handle not just money, but everything else as well. Everything. And while we're at it—*everybody.*

Professional acrobats, skaters, and dancers model this idea in their work. At the top level of their sports, they perform spins and flips at speeds and frequencies that would leave the average person incapacitated with dizziness. And yet somehow they still manage to land precision jumps or skate within inches of the rink wall at full speed. They maintain perfect control over their bodies. Acquiring those moves is their business. But once acquired, those moves impact their sense of balance, affecting everything else they do. Can you imagine what it takes to spin like a blur and then land a triple Lutz? Or twirl across the floor on the tips of your ballet shoes without flying off the stage? Those athletes train themselves to handle the dizzying influences of the moves they perform. They learn techniques to adjust their perceptions and compensate for the effects generated when they perform their routines. They practice "spotting" as a way to maintain a point of reference. They learn to feel their balance with their feet instead of just their inner ears. Over time, they become experts at neutralizing the factors that distort their senses.

Money has a dizzying effect on its holders as well. And if you don't learn how to master that factor first, everything else about your involvement with money will be distorted and a little bit out of balance. This explains why so many people stumble and fall when they come into wealth suddenly. So the first part of learning how to be rich involves similar training. The key, as the old saying goes, is to possess money without it possessing you.

In fact, a New Testament contributor, known primarily as the apostle Paul, made this very point. Paul was a mentor to a younger man named Timothy. And in effect, he gave Timothy lessons on this very subject. It wasn't because Timothy had a large estate. But as a young pastor, Timothy was in charge of preaching to people in places like Ephesus. By this time, many rich people had embraced Jesus and his teachings. Churches were popping up in many of the port cities that ringed the Mediterranean. Port cities were epicenters of trade and wealth. Paul, who had planted many of these churches, knew that rich people faced unique challenges as they adopted the new worldview introduced through Christianity. Just like today, the Christians of Paul's time were vulnerable to the dizzying effects of money. So he addressed some of their specific needs in a letter to his young protégé. Paul wrote:

> Command those who are rich in this present world not
> to be arrogant nor to put their hope in wealth, which is
> so uncertain ... *(1 Timothy 6:17)*

These twenty-four words are saturated with implication and insight. Timothy knew this. He understood his responsibility to unpack this treasure chest of information for the churches he would visit. In the paragraphs and pages that follow, I will attempt to do the same for you.

MONEY DOES

The first point embedded in this message goes back to something we've already pointed out. Namely, money does things to people. People who are rich have tendencies and propensities that are unique to them. Those tendencies can be attributed directly to the presence of riches in their lives. The more a person possesses, the greater his potential to acquire a distorted sense of reality and the greater the odds that he will lose his sense of balance. So Paul instructs Timothy to do what he can to neutralize the effects of wealth on the wealthy.

Specifically, Paul writes, money does two things to people: It makes us arrogant, and over time it becomes our primary source of hope, leaving us with the impression that we are self-sufficient. Wealth has its own gravitational pull. It will always draw those who have it in the direction of those two things. It is in this way that wealth eventually possesses its possessors. Cross a river, and the current will pull you in a downstream direction. Cross paths with wealth and you will be drawn in the direction of arrogance and the illusion of self-sufficiency. To survive the test of wealth, to be good at being rich, one must learn to compensate and resist its sinister force.

Money leaves us with the impression that we are self-sufficient.

So let's talk about arrogance. Ever met any arrogant rich people? Oh yeah. That one's not hard to imagine, is it? The definition of *arrogant* is "having an inflated sense of self-worth." So it's easy to see why rich people would lean in this direction. When your *net worth* is inflated, it only makes sense that your *self-worth* should be inflated too. Human nature tells us that our identities are defined by our possessions. That started in high school, didn't it? Early on we learned that we are the sum of what we own.

Hey, guys, remember your new basketball shoes? You couldn't wait for people to notice them, even though you acted like you didn't notice they were noticing. Remember how much better you felt about yourself when you were rockin' those two overpriced slabs of rubber, string, glue, and a swoosh stitched on the side? Ladies, remember ... Well, I have no idea what you remember. But I'm sure you remember something you wore or owned in high school that made you walk a little taller or swing a little more noticeably.

And we all remember the opposite as well. That *car* your dad drove. That *house* you would never invite your friends to. Well, actually, that house you used to invite your friends to until you saw your friend's house. So yeah, the propensity to measure our value by the value of our things started early. And to some extent, we never fully recovered.

If you have only a little, you tend to feel "little" and unimportant compared to people who are richer—especially in a culture that puts so much emphasis on material things. As your estate grows, however, your sense of self-worth tends to grow right along with it. Strange, isn't it? Makes no sense at all.

It's not just overall self-worth either. Rich people tend to see themselves as superior in each of the categories that make up self-worth. When you're rich, there's an inclination to see yourself as smarter, better looking, and more competent. And the people around you generally reinforce this myth. As mentioned earlier, when rich people have ideas, everybody is inclined to think they're good ideas. Ideas just sound better when rich people suggest them.

Money apparently alters one's appearance as well. Have you ever met someone, discovered she was rich, and then she seemed a little better looking than when you first met her? Or at least a little *less unattractive*?

At any rate, the richer people are, the more attention we give them. Our inclination is to have a little more respect for the opinions they share, the decisions they make, and the shoes they are stylin'. So, is it any wonder that people who have a lot of money—who are constantly surrounded by people bowing and scraping to their superior self-worth—would, over time, begin to see themselves differently? It just goes with the territory.

THE MIGRATION OF HOPE

But that's not all money does to its possessors. In this same passage, Paul warned Timothy about a second tendency for rich people. And this one is even worse than the first. According to Paul, when you're rich there's a natural inclination for your hope to migrate toward money. And if you fall into this trap, then the wealthier you get, the more you will hope in riches.

At first that might not sound like much of a problem. After all, there always seems to be a greater sense of hope if there's a pile of money available to you. Where there's money, there's hope. Things are more hopeful when you know you can pay the bills, save for the future, and even have some left over to share. Hope often accompanies riches. That's just a fact.

But placing your hope *in* riches is something different. And that's where Paul draws an important line. It's one thing to have hope *and* riches at the same time. But it's another thing to have hope *in* riches. When riches become the basis for your hope—the source of it—you're headed down a slippery slope.

When riches become the basis for your hope – the source of it – you're headed down a slippery slope.

Naturally, none of us believe we're guilty of this. People generally assume they won't cross the line. Or they're not rich enough to worry about it in the first place. But even if you've got a basic savings account, a 401(k), or an insurance policy — if you've engaged in even the most basic steps of financial planning — you're standing in the river with the current pulling you toward self-sufficiency. I'm not saying we shouldn't have plans that involve money. I'm just saying that when we do, we need to compensate for the effect money will have on us.

Years ago, there was a church secretary named Ella who was a source of joy to everyone in the congregation. She had a great sense of humor that always lifted the staff's morale. She was especially liked by the children in the church. She took time to greet them by name and offered them candy from the bowl she kept stocked on her desk. She was a favorite with the young people, and they always called out her name when they saw her in the halls.

But one year a change came over Ella. A haggard gaze replaced her warm smile. Her sense of humor went away, and she adopted a matter-of-fact posture in conversations. Children called her name in the hallways expecting her enthusiastic reply, but she only grunted or ignored them altogether. She would even snap at them for being too loud. She was nothing short of an ornery curmudgeon.

Finally, one of the little boys in the church asked his mother what was wrong with Ella. The mother explained that after more than thirty years with his company, Ella's husband had been laid off just eleven months shy of retirement. He lost his salary, his benefits, and his pension. He'd spent his entire career with that company. And on the brink of the payoff, they had left him high and dry. It was a heartless, cutthroat move. But the economy was tough, and lots of other companies were doing the same.

Ella felt betrayed. In all her life, she'd never imagined someone treating her family so cruelly. Her worldview was shattered. And her source of joy was shattered along with it.

Ella was a solid Christian. But without realizing it, her hope had migrated to riches. She and her husband weren't millionaires. Not even close. But as his retirement neared, she had begun to count down the days. She was really looking forward to it. She pictured herself continuing to work for the church for at least another ten years. And with her husband free to volunteer as well, their days promised to be even more fulfilling. She'd drawn up a budget that would enable them to travel while they were still young enough to get around. With the money from his pension, they wouldn't have to worry about going hungry in their old age. It was only a modest retirement package—not too much to ask for a lifetime of loyal service to the company.

When the money went away, Ella's hope went with it. She was still a Christian. She hoped in Christ for salvation. But she didn't know how to hope for anything else anymore.

So here's the challenge. Financial stewardship and

planning are important. We're supposed to be responsible with our money. We need to address things like life insurance, savings, and retirement. We just need to figure out how to do it without putting our hope in riches.

For poor people, that's easy. They don't struggle with putting their hope in riches. For them, money has proven to be a poor source of hope. If anything, they know firsthand how it can let you down. They've learned that money runs out. So unless you want your hope to run out too, you'd better find a different source for it.

Proverbs 18:11 describes the migration of hope this way: "The wealth of the rich is their fortified city; they imagine it a wall too high to scale."

In other words, rich people (which includes us, remember) have the potential to reach a point where they see money as the source of their safety and security. When somebody has a good income, there's a tendency to get caught up in a paycheck or a bank account. When something threatens a rich person's way of life, he can just write a check or swipe a credit card and neutralize the threat. Whatever he needs is within his reach—thanks to money. Like a high wall, money forms an invisible perimeter around him, giving him the spending power to keep trouble at bay. Food, shelter, transportation, health care, entertainment: if he needs something, he just buys it. Riches let him do that.

And the writer of Proverbs observes that when things are going well financially—and we're experiencing a long string of situations in which we've needed something and all we had to do was reach for our wallets—our hope will tend to migrate. If we repeat this pattern long enough, we will form an association in our minds between hope and money. Eventually, we will begin to imagine that there is an amount of money large enough to take care of us for life.

Notice that the writer of that proverb said the rich "imagine" a wall too high to scale. The wall exists only in their imaginations. In reality, there's no amount of money that can protect us from everything.

There's no amount of money that can protect us from everything.

That explains why Ella was hit so hard by her financial setback. Planning for retirement was the wise thing for her to do. But there was a fatal flaw in Ella's thinking. Somewhere along the way, she began to imagine an amount of money that she and her husband needed for retirement. And in her mind, that money was the key to their provision throughout retirement. Over time, all her hope had migrated to that wealth.

The richer you get, the deeper you fall into this trap. CNBC reporter Robert Frank observed the very same thing among the *über*-rich. In his book *Richistan*, Frank investigates families that create their own self-sustaining civilizations, "complete with their own health-care system (concierge doctors), travel network (Net Jets, destination clubs), separate economy (double-digit income gains and double-digit inflation), and language ('Who's your house-hold manager?')."

It's interesting that no matter how sophisticated their mini-civilizations are, the *über*-rich still manage to feel insecure. Years ago, Sandra and I had dinner with a billionaire couple. We knew they were billionaires because it had been all over the news a few weeks earlier when they sold a company for billions of dollars. While we were having conversation, this couple began talking about all the economic threats we face today. And with a very serious tone, they remarked about how you have to be really careful with your money because there's just no end to the ways you can lose it. Their concern was sincere. And their fear was authentic.

When it was over, Sandra and I just looked at each other and silently communicated what we were thinking: *If the billionaires are worried about money, then we're in big trouble!* That couple was right about one thing. There are lots of needs that even a billion dollars can't meet.

You don't have to be a Christian to get behind this principle. We've all seen that it doesn't work to count on money for your hope. Like the MasterCard commercial admits, "There are some things money can't buy." It can't buy the priceless things in life. And there comes a time when it can't buy hope either. Because there's no amount of money that can guarantee you hope in any and all circumstances.

Therefore, putting your hope in riches is a dangerous trap. And Jesus knew all about this threat. That's why he had more to say about money and possessions than heaven and hell combined.

Proverbs goes on to paint a picture of what can happen when our hope migrates. In fact, the writer concludes that he would rather *not* be rich so as to avoid this threat. He says, "Give me neither poverty nor riches, but give me only my daily bread. Otherwise, I may have too much and disown you and say, 'Who is the LORD?'" (Proverbs 30:8–9).

Which brings us back to Paul's warning about the potential of riches to dislodge the hope we're supposed to place in God. And here's the real danger in that: If we allow our hope to migrate toward riches, we'll start to hoard. Consider this: When our billionaire friends start rehearsing all the things that could go wrong, are they more likely or less likely to be generous? Are they more likely or less likely to hoard—just in case something happens? And since there's no amount that can guarantee safety, they'll be stuck in that loop for the rest of their lives. Remember, rich people give away a smaller percentage than poor people.

That's how *not* to be rich.

I WILL NOT TRUST IN RICHES

Wealth has some pretty powerful side effects. If wealth were an over-the-counter medicine, there would be bold warnings printed on the packaging. *Warning: May cause arrogance. While taking this medicine, extra precaution should be taken not to offend people. If taken for prolonged periods, may impair perception, causing hope to migrate.* If you saw a commercial for wealth on TV, it would show pictures of happy people holding hands in the park. Meanwhile, the announcer would be listing all the ways it can ruin your kidneys, rot your stomach, cause sudden heart failure, and destroy your life.

So what can you do to offset these terrible side effects?

With some medicines, the side effects can be reduced by taking them with food, by starting off with small doses, or by combining them with additional drugs. The side effects of wealth can be mitigated in a similar way. Not by drinking milk, but by exercising a particular routine on a regular basis. Paul explained it to Timothy this way:

> Command those who are rich in this present world not to be arrogant nor to put their hope in wealth, which is so uncertain, but to put their hope in God, who richly provides us with everything for our enjoyment. *(1 Timothy 6:17)*

Did you see it? The way to offset the side effects of wealth ... to avoid being arrogant and putting your hope in wealth ... is to put your hope in God. That's the short answer anyway. We'll get to the step-by-step plan in a moment.

Haven't you met people who are good at this? There are some rich people who, no matter how much God sends their way, never seem to put their hope in their riches. Some are "middle-class" rich. Some are multimillionaires. And some only seem rich when you compare them to a third-world country. But no matter how rich they are, they don't trust in their riches. They trust in God.

An amazing thing can be observed within this group of rich people. Since their hope is in the Lord, they never seem to suffer from the first thing Paul cautioned about: arrogance. Despite being rich, they're humble and thankful and generous at heart. They don't worry if they'll have enough or if the stock market will recover or if the merger will go through. Their hope is in the Lord. So their hope remains steady in every circumstance they face.

So what's the connection? How do they do it? What do you *do* in order to put your hope in God? What are the steps?

Look at what Paul says next:

Command them to do good, to be rich in good deeds, and to be generous and willing to share. *(1 Timothy 6:18)*

There you go. A step-by-step plan for keeping your hope from migrating. If you think about it, adhering to that command would definitely have an impact on things. Imagine if every rich person were to live by that statement. It would be hard to be arrogant if you spent all your time thinking up things to do that were "good." And you couldn't "be rich in good deeds, and ... generous and willing to share" if you also put all your hope in the things you were so generously sharing.

I have a simple mantra that sums it all up. I like mantras because they summarize big ideas into little phrases that are easy to remember. So are you ready? Here it is:

"I will not trust in riches but in him who richly provides."

Go ahead. Say that out loud to yourself a couple of times. If you're sitting alone in a Starbucks, adjust your Bluetooth headset first and nobody will even know you're talking to yourself.

That one simple shift of your mindset holds the key to being good at being rich. Wealth has side effects. And the side effects that come with wealth are the very things that keep us from being good at it. Ironic, isn't it? The richer you get, the harder it gets to be good at it. But if we can address the temptation to trust in riches, "I will not trust in riches," and reinforce the idea of trusting in God instead, "but in him who richly provides," we will neutralize the side effects.

Sounds pretty simple. Just repeat that handy phrase to yourself a couple times a day and you're set—"I will not trust in riches but in him who richly provides."

So if that's all it takes be good at being rich, then why aren't more people good at it?

As it turns out, there's a crucial pitfall that trips people up. And as we're about to see next, it begins with a simple false assumption about the things you possess.

Chapter 3

CONSUMPTION ASSUMPTION

If your desires be endless, your cares and fears will be so too.

Thomas Fuller

J ust a few months into the Civil War, a sobering reality began to dampen the American psyche. Prior to the war, many were actually looking forward to the fight. America had been founded on strong convictions, and fighting for your beliefs seemed noble and meaningful. But it was soon obvious that each side had underestimated the other and had miscalculated the price that had to be paid in order to settle the conflict. After several major battles and staggering losses of life, the enormity of the undertaking hung over both the North and the South like dark clouds. Any trace of cavalier arrogance that had existed at the outset of the war had long since drowned in the rivers of blood that flowed from the battlefields.

For President Abraham Lincoln, his responsibility in all of this was obvious. Southern leaders had seceded from the United States, essentially stealing half the country for themselves. And it was Lincoln's job to go down there and get it back.

To accomplish this daunting task, he began amassing an army capable of overrunning the rebels that now occupied land as far north as Virginia. To command his army, Lincoln chose George B. McClellan, a man who seemed as foreboding and competent as the massive Army of the Potomac that he commanded. One of Lincoln's aides described McClellan this way:

> He is the impersonation of health and strength, and he is in the prime of early manhood. His uniform is fault-less and his stars are brilliant, especially the middle one on each strap. His face is full of intelligence, of will-power, of self-assertion, and he, too, is in some respects a born leader of men. He has been admirably educated for such duties as are now upon him, and he has studied the science and art of war among European camps and forts and armies and battlefields. He has vast stores of technical knowledge never to be acquired by any man among the backwoods, or on the prairies, or in law courts, or in political conventions.

Right away, McClellan showed an amazing talent for taking average men and turning them into an army. His discipline was downright inspiring. As a result, when the massive Army of the Potomac was training for battle in the Virginia countryside, spectators would often gather to witness the spectacle of sheer force. After one such public review, Julia Ward Howe was so inspired that upon returning to her hotel room, she penned the lyrics to "The Battle Hymn of the Republic." That's how impressive McClellan was. He had taken the raw material of civilian volunteers and forged them into a legion that outnumbered his counterpart nearly three to one and whose poise and conviction evoked images of the army of God.

Though the North had been defeated at Bull Run under the leadership of McClellan's predecessor, now they had regrouped. Under McClellan, it appeared they were finally bringing their A-game. Their war machine was cranked up and pumping a steady supply of resources to the front lines outside of Washington. Tactically, the North held a tremendous advantage. As their military might grew, the tide shifted in their favor. And it was generally understood that the sooner the Union army attacked, the less resistance they would face. Momentum and timing were critical. A decisive initiative launched early could bring a quick conclusion to the war. But McClellan waited.

At first, his inaction seemed prudent and strategic. During July and August of 1861, he attended important meetings with Lincoln and other military leaders in Washington. He was biding his time, collecting intelligence, and creating a battle plan as glorious as his army. August turned into September as the army continued to strengthen. October came, filled with drills and discussions, but not a single dispatch. The window of opportunity was slowly closing.

A group of senators visited the White House to report the mounting concern felt among the country's leaders. So in late October, Lincoln paid a personal visit to McClellan to learn when they might expect a move by the commander. McClellan responded by requesting more men and equipment. Despite the fact that his army already outnumbered the rebels, he seemed to be pursuing an advantage so great that the South might simply surrender from intimidation.

McClellan's near-pacifist war strategy was in stark contrast to that of the Union leaders who had appointed him. In essence, a war-within-a-war broke out between McClellan and his superiors as they argued about the appropriate sense of urgency for the situation. McClellan refused to rush. Congress demanded action. And Lincoln modeled patience and grace as his own frustration with McClellan grew. "I cannot move on [the Confederates] with as great a force as they have," McClellan once argued. But his critics saw things differently. One Lincoln aide wrote, "The simple truth is, there was never an hour during General McClellan's command of the army that he had not more troops than he knew what to do with; yet he was always instinctively calling for more."

On one hand, McClellan expressed a sense of personal responsibility for the well-being of his troops. "The Army of the Potomac is my army as much as any army ever belonged to the man that created it," he once said. "I say it with the earnestness of a general who feels in his heart the loss of every brave man ... I have seen too many dead and wounded comrades."

On the surface McClellan was serving the Union. But underneath it all, his sense of personal responsibility for the army was slowly turning into a sense of ownership. He was intrigued by his own power. In a letter to his wife, he gushed, "By some strange operation of magic, I seem to have become the power of the land. I almost think that were I to win some small success now I could become dictator or anything else that might please me." One historian described him as "a vain and unstable man, with considerable military knowledge, who sat on a horse well and wanted to be President." Another concluded, "He believed himself to be God's chosen instrument for saving the Union. When he lost the courage to fight, as he did in every battle, he believed he was preserving his army to fight the next time on another and better day."

McClellan's courage was questioned on the battlefield as well. Historians describe "McClellan's absence from the field of battle during major engagements and a predisposition to allow subordinates to make crucial decisions on the battlefield."

All winter long, the delays continued. December. January. February. March. Finally in April he began a timid campaign, laying siege to Yorktown against a handful of rebels posing as a larger army. The regiment from the North outnumbered the Southerners ten to one. But the rebels presented logs painted black to resemble cannons. They moved back and forth to create the illusion of multiple companies. Completely fooled, McClellan only cowered behind his own entrenchments.

Throughout 1862, the pattern seemed to repeat itself: Washington pushed for action. But McClellan commanded from his own set of perceptions.

The last straw came at Antietam. It could easily have been a rout for McClellan's army, except that he withheld nearly a fourth of his troops throughout the battle, allowing the Confederates to refortify after each Yankee advance. McClellan's indecision resulted in the bloodiest day of the war.

The pugnacious leader Winston Churchill once reflected, "McClellan for all his qualities of leadership lacked the final ounces of fighting spirit." However, history suggests that it wasn't so much a lack of courage that limited McClellan but a sense of self-importance that caused him to lose sight of the cause he was supposed to be serving.

In the midst of the McClellan debacle, Lincoln visited the army as they encamped near Antietam. He was accompanied by Illinois Secretary of State Ozias M. Hatch, who recorded the scene in vivid detail. "Early next morning, I was awakened by Mr. Lincoln. It was very early—daylight was just lighting the east—the soldiers were all asleep in their tents," he wrote. "Scarce a sound could be heard except the notes of early birds, and the farm-yard voices from the distant farms. Lincoln said to me, 'Come, Hatch, I want you to take a walk with me.'"

As the two reached a clearing, they paused to take in the moment. The camp was stirring to life. The President fixed a deliberate gaze across the sea of tents, and then finally he waved his hand across the scene as if ready to pronounce an unspoken commentary or a nonverbal State of the Union. As he did, he leaned toward Hatch and in what was almost a whisper asked, "Hatch—Hatch, what is all this?"

"Why, Mr. Lincoln, this is the Army of the Potomac," Hatch replied.

Another moment passed as Lincoln formed his thoughts. Then, he took a decisive breath and declared in a louder voice, "No, Hatch, no. This is General McClellan's bodyguard."

According to Hatch, nothing more was said. The two simply returned to their tents. And a few weeks later, McClellan was removed from his post.[4]

---

4. See Ethan S. Rafuse, *Abraham Lincoln and George B. McClellan*, www.abrahamlincolnsclassroom.org/Library/newsletter.asp?ID=129&CRLI=177.

FAULTY THINKING

McClellan was the model general except for one thing. He embraced a simple false assumption about the army of men he led: he thought it was *his* army.

As a result, he never quite managed to serve the true objective of the war. He concerned himself with many things, but somehow he failed to concern himself with engaging the enemy. Despite commanding one of the most formidable armies ever assembled, he served less important objectives — like his own survival. As generals go, McClellan was beyond rich. He possessed more than most commanders could ever dream about. He had everything he needed, but he lost sight of what he needed them for.

McClellan was not that different from today's rich Americans. We possess more than most people around the world and throughout history could ever dream about. We have everything we need. But we lose sight of what we need it for.

We have everything we need. But we lose sight of what we need it for.

Jesus taught his followers a rather interesting definition of *greed*. He said that greed is the assumption that everything placed in our hands is for our consumption. Brilliant, isn't it? You've probably known people who had lots of things in their hands, but that wasn't what made them seem greedy. Nor was it when they kept some of those things for themselves. It was when they went a step further and thought everything they owned was intended for them.

The scene where Jesus taught this concept is recorded in the gospel of Luke. One day when Jesus was preaching to his followers, an argument broke out in the crowd. It was an argument about greed. One person accused the other of greed and vice versa. In response, Jesus began to tell a story:

> The ground of a certain rich man yielded an abundant harvest ... *(Luke 12:16)*

So far, Jesus could just as well have been describing a middle-class American in our times. Here's a rich guy who finds himself with more than he needs. He had a good year. Perhaps he closed a big deal or launched a successful product or opened a new store in the mall. And now the money's rolling in. So what will he do with the extra?

Remember, Jesus is making up the story. He could have had the guy do anything he wanted. Jesus wanted to get us thinking about the different things we could do when we find ourselves in that situation. He wanted to teach us the right and wrong ways to respond if we ever find ourselves with more than we need. He showed us how to be good at being rich. And interestingly enough, the rich guy in Jesus' story did what a lot of us do when we have good years. Jesus continued:

> He thought to himself, "What shall I do? I have no place to store my crops." *(Luke 12:17)*

Just put yourself in his place. It's that Saturday morning when you wake up with no place to be. There's money in the bank and gas in the tank. For a split second, you think about how to spend the day. Home Depot? The movie theater? Your favorite restaurant? What shall I do today? Or it's the moment when your tax refund arrives in the mail. You weren't expecting it. So what should you do with it? Upgrade your computer? Trade in your car? Buy new curtains? Put it in the college fund? Jesus went on:

> Then he said, "This is what I'll do. I will tear down my barns and build bigger ones, and there I will store my surplus grain. And I'll say to myself, 'You have plenty of grain laid up for many years. Take life easy; eat, drink and be merry.'" *(Luke 12:18–19)*

Ahhh. But of course. Jesus is teaching about saving. Or if the guy in the story worked in agriculture, maybe Jesus is saying we should invest our surplus. Possibly start our own business. Those certainly sound like the suggestions we'd expect from a wise teacher.

So the rich man in the story tore down his old barns and built new ones. It's such a smart move that our government will even give you a tax write-off if you do that today. At first glance, that seems pretty reasonable. In fact, it's industrious. Good for him. He had a good year, so he ought to do what people do when things go their way, right? Pay off their debts. Max out their Roth IRAs and their profit sharing. Put some away in a savings account. Maybe even reward themselves with new clothes or flat-screen TVs, or trade in their old cars.

So far, it's just a good story. We like the premise and we like the main character. We're living vicariously through his season of good fortune. This story has the potential to be the feel-good movie of the summer. We're just waiting for Jesus to say, "And he lived happily ever after." But then things took a morbid turn:

> But God said to him, "You fool! This very night your life will be demanded from you. Then who will get what you have prepared for yourself?" This is how it will be with whoever stores up things for themselves but is not rich toward God. *(Luke 12:20–21)*

Ouch. Talk about your unexpected downers. Suddenly, the guy dies. That must have gotten the attention of Jesus' audience. No doubt it was disturbing for some. Maybe a few people in the crowd inwardly celebrated out of jealousy. But at any rate, Jesus wasn't just trying to entertain them. He was making a point. Because that surprising twist in the rich man's story directly mirrors a surprising twist we can expect in our own stories—if we fail to heed Jesus' message. It's not that we'll die the night after we get a raise. But if we only do with our extra money as the rich man did, there will come a time—suddenly—when we discover the foolishness of our actions.

A MORE SECURE HOPE

Like most things Jesus had to say, this parable represented a monumental shift from conventional thinking. He was announcing a new paradigm for those times when we find ourselves with extra.

Whenever we have more than we need, our natural assumption will be that it's for our own consumption. But that's the wrong mindset. And in his practical way, Jesus was exposing the flaw in that way of thinking. If we simply store up for ourselves and are not rich toward God, then everything we possess will be a total loss. At some point, everybody leaves it all behind. But if we will take advantage of the times when we have more than we need — and do more than simply save it for ourselves — then we can become rich toward God. And the implication is that it won't be a loss anymore.

At some point, everybody leaves it all behind.

When you overlay Jesus' teaching on top of Paul's commands for rich people, we get a plan for avoiding this pitfall. There's a set of things to avoid:

... not to be arrogant nor to put their hope in wealth ...

And there's a set of things to pursue:

... to put their hope in God ... to do good, to be rich in good deeds, and to be generous and willing to share.

To keep from becoming arrogant ... to keep your hope from migrating ... and to sidestep the assumption that everything is for your consumption, you are to pursue a life of generosity. It's not just a good thing to do. It's not some tip for how to be a good person. It's a preventative for the side effects of wealth.

But what exactly does it mean "to do good, to be rich in good deeds ... to be generous and willing to share" and to be "rich toward God"? We'll talk about that next.

Chapter 4

PLANNING AHEAD

*When I have money, I get rid of it
quickly, lest it find a way
into my heart.*

John Wesley

In 1783, Edward Jenner had a crazy idea. All over Europe, smallpox lurked like a bogeyman. It was one of the biggest killers of the day, bringing death to nearly 80 percent of the children who caught it. When news of an outbreak was reported, families waited helplessly to find out who would come down with the deadly boils next, and mothers nervously secluded their children to protect them from exposure.

But Jenner had a different approach. He believed it was possible to take steps to make a person immune to the disease — to go toward the problem instead of hiding from it. English folklore told of milkmaids who couldn't catch smallpox if they'd already been sick with "cowpox," a weaker version of smallpox carried by cows. So, Jenner's idea was to expose people to the fluid from an active cowpox boil — on purpose! And sure enough, all who followed Jenner's treatment seemed untouchable, no matter how severe the outbreak around them.

In his medical papers, Jenner invented a new word, *vaccine*, based on the Latin word for cow, *vacca*. Some of the nastiest diseases in the world are now under control thanks to the use of vaccines — including influenza. And it all traces back to the work of Jenner.

For affluent people today, there's a threat as devastating as smallpox was in Jenner's time. It's called *affluenza*. As we've seen already, it's rampant too. It causes bouts of arrogance and chronic dislocated hope. The symptoms aren't always obvious either. They sneak up on you like an invisible growth that goes undetected while it eats away your insides.

THREE Ps IN A POD

But as Paul taught, there's a way to immunize against affluenza. No matter how rich you get, you can protect yourself from the negative side effects of wealth. The antidote is another word that also comes from Latin: *generosity.*

The problem with a word like *generosity* is that it's as hard to define as the word *rich.* In fact, just as nobody thinks he's rich, *everybody* thinks he's generous. I mean, nobody thinks he's stingy or greedy. *Generous* is one of those words that's open to interpretation. And that's one of the reasons rich people are so bad at being rich. There's no real grading system for it. It's like PE class in high school. You're pretty much guaranteed a passing grade just for having a body. In the same way, if you've ever given a dollar to a homeless person, or directions to a tourist, or a smile to a stranger, you can rightfully consider yourself generous.

That may be true. But it won't help you demonstrate the kind of generosity that vaccinates you against the side effects of wealth. For that, we need something a little more tangible. We need guidelines to follow. We need principles to observe. We need prescriptions to take.

When you take everything Jesus taught about being generous and distill it down, three common themes emerge. There may be more than that, but these three ideas give us a great picture of what it looks like to be generous and to neutralize the side effects of wealth. I call them the three Ps.

PRIORITY GIVING

The first P stands for *priority*. The key to Jenner's vaccination was to apply the technique *before* an outbreak occurred. And the same is true with generosity. It won't happen unless you make it a *priority*. If you wait until you're rich, you'll never start, because rich people live in denial that they're rich. No matter how rich or poor you might feel, *right now* is the time to be generous.

Now wait a minute, I know what you're thinking. *Right now* means *soon*, right? You're thinking that if I knew the details of your financial situation, I would never advise you to start being generous. That wouldn't make sense. You have a handful of important issues to address first, like getting out of debt, repairing your broken-down car, paying for braces, and getting caught up on your cell phone bill. Generosity isn't just for rich people, but surely it's not for broke people, right?

Actually, generosity isn't dependent on your finances at all. As counterintuitive as it seems, generosity begins wherever you are. That's what it means to make it a *priority*.

Generosity begins wherever you are.

Priorities are funny things. We know they're important. We *want* to keep them in order. But there's always something rising up to challenge them. Important things. The thought of standing your ground and saying no to something important is scary. It takes courage to pull it off. What if the payoff never comes? To keep something a priority, you have to be able to stay on course even when everything inside you might be screaming to go in the other direction.

Think about the vaccinations Jenner gave. There's something unnatural about exposing yourself to the elements of a deadly disease on purpose. Imagine how Jenner's first patients must have felt. They were perfectly healthy. They had managed to avoid the disease. They were probably thinking the avoidance method was working pretty well. Why change? But instead of sticking with that plan, Jenner suggested that they import a diseased sample from another town and infect themselves with it. Keep this in mind: In Jenner's day, vaccinations didn't just make your arm sore for a few days. You got a full-blown illness. It wasn't the deadly version of the virus that caused smallpox, but cowpox was a pretty nasty illness too. And they didn't have Advil back then either. Can you imagine the courage and foresight it took to sign up for that?

It takes the same kind of foresight and courage to make generosity your priority. The time to start doing it is when it seems to make the least sense. There's a tendency to think that generosity is for when you have extra money, when you're rich. And like we've been saying, you probably don't think you're rich. And since you're not rich, why would you give away what little you have? Isn't that like exposing yourself to a deadly disease when you're already sick?

When you make giving a priority, something happens inside of you. Especially when it's financially challenging to do so. It's like you loosen your grip on a value system whose motto says, "Money is the key to life and happiness and safety." In that split second, you reject that way of thinking for one that says, "My hope is not in riches but in him who richly provides." And suddenly, your eyes begin to open to a value system that can't be measured by dollars.

The best way to make giving a priority is to make it the very first check you write every month. Before the mortgage. Before groceries or clothing. Before saving. Whenever God blesses you with income, let your first action be a gesture that acknowledges where it came from. Whatever the amount, do it first. The minute you deposit your paycheck. This not only ensures that you'll guard it as a priority, but it's a symbolic way of reminding you where your hope lies.

PERCENTAGE GIVING

The second P stands for *percentage*. In chapter 1, I shared some statistics that show how the richer we get, the less we give away. It's incredible, isn't it? The more *extra* money we get, the less we view it as extra. Of course, we tell ourselves that we're giving more because the dollar amount goes up.

But in terms of percentages, giving actually goes down. It's almost sinister how this tendency creeps into our behaviors and derails our efforts to be good at being rich.

If you want to guard against the side effects of wealth, you can't evaluate your giving in terms of dollars. Percentages give you a much better reflection of whether you have control of your money or your money has control of you.

Everybody's entrusted with a portion in this life. We don't all get the same amount. So it doesn't make sense to measure generosity based on the ability to give a certain dollar figure. If Warren Buffet gives $1,000 to charity, can he be sure he's protected from the side effects of wealth?

Jesus taught this very principle to his followers. Back in those days, the offering plate wasn't passed. It sat in the same place and people walked up and dropped in their coins where everyone could see. Jesus was watching as person after person came up to make his offering. It was a real cross section of the community. There were rich people who put in larger donations and poor people who put in what they could. As Jesus looked on, he took note of the rich people. They wore fancy clothes, groomed their beards like teenage girls getting ready for school, and paraded around like ornaments in a menagerie. Not to mention, they took advantage of widows along the way. Jesus said they "devour widows' houses."

All of a sudden, an elderly widow hobbled up to the offering plate and produced two small copper coins. It was almost embarrassing how insignificant her donation was, especially compared to all of the successful, prosperous people who came before her. The woman was obviously dirt poor. Jesus' comments on the scene are recorded in the gospel of Mark:

> Calling his disciples to him, Jesus said, "Truly I tell you, this poor widow has put more into the treasury than all the others. They all gave out of their wealth; but she, out of her poverty, put in everything—all she had to live on." *(Mark 12:43–44)*

If you've heard this story before, it's easy to miss what it says about percentage giving. At first glance, the message is warm and uplifting because Jesus is showing favor to someone with whom we sympathize. There's even a group of antagonists in the story who are being mean to old widows ("devour[ing]" their houses) while primping themselves and showing off for one another. Who isn't pulling for the poor, old woman in this story? It could be your grandma. It makes us feel good to see Jesus, God's Son, giving a shout-out to the little people.

The emotional takeaway of this story is that Jesus is kind toward little old ladies. But the passage contains a powerful principle about giving too. And it's this: The percentage matters more than the sum. The money principle doesn't give us warm fuzzies like the part about little old ladies does. But it's just as significant.

The percentage matters more than the sum.

That story gives us one of the earliest portraits of rich people who are bad at being rich. They're arrogant. Their hope and preoccupation have migrated to their stuff. And they act like everything they possess is for their own consumption. The side effects of wealth have taken over. Meanwhile, the widow is faithfully practicing generosity.

So what percentage should you give? I tell people to start with 10 percent because the Bible writers have a lot to say about the *tithe*, which means "tenth." For some people, that's extremely uncomfortable. But so is a colonoscopy, and those save countless lives. It just depends on how badly you want to protect yourself from the side effects of wealth. Remember, it's not just a way to be "good." It's a preventative. The most important thing is to start somewhere. Even if it's just 1 percent.

PROGRESSIVE GIVING

The third P stands for *progressive*. If you really want to guard yourself against the side effects of wealth, you shouldn't overlook this one. To be progressive simply means that over time you raise the percentage. If you've been giving the same 10 percent even as your income grows, bump it up to 11 percent, then 12 percent, and so on.

Here's why. It's kind of like when bacteria become tolerant of antibiotics, rendering them ineffective. As you vaccinate yourself against the side effects of wealth over the years, those preventatives don't have quite the same effect.

Let's say your first job pays $20,000 a year. As a priority, percentage giver, you give away $2,000 — 10 percent! That's a lot of money to someone making $20,000. Think of the impact that must have on your heart. Is arrogance likely to be a problem in that scenario? Will your hope migrate to your money? Hardly.

But fast-forward a decade or two. Now you're making $200,000 a year. The kids are grown. The house is paid off. And your 401(k) holds enough for a comfortable retirement. If you're still giving 10 percent, that's a whopping $20,000 a year. But if you need only $50,000 to live on, that still leaves you with $130,000 extra! First of all, congratulations! You've been a faithful giver, and you've maintained a lifestyle that gives you financial margin. As for the side effects of wealth, however, you might not be doing so well. That's a lot of extra money lying around. It's a breeding ground for tiny arrogant thoughts. And with so much money to throw at any problem that arises, you might be tempted to forget where your hope lies.

The solution? As your financial situation changes throughout life, change your giving percentage along with it. When you make that initial adjustment to giving 10 percent, it soon becomes comfortable. And while financial comfort is generally a good thing, it can also make you more vulnerable to the side effects of wealth. That's when it's time to bump up your vaccination a bit. If you've been giving the same percentage for most of your life, consider raising it. Life is not stagnant. It's progressive in nature. And your giving should be progressive too.

Life is not stagnant. It's progressive in nature.
And your giving should be progressive too.

LIFE BEFORE VACCINATIONS

Before Jenner introduced his vaccinations, there was no preventive medicine for smallpox. All you could do was react when it happened. But Jenner gave us a new option. For the first time, we could develop a *plan* for smallpox. In the same way, planning is the key to managing the side effects of wealth.

Generosity isn't just something you ought to do. It's the vaccination against allowing hope to migrate, becoming arrogant, and basically being bad at being rich. Generosity isn't just something you do when you have more. It's something you practice constantly so you'll know what to do when you have more. It's part of a plan, not just an overflow of the heart. It's a preventative against the side effects of being rich.

In fact, if you approach giving in any other way, it will always seem unnatural. If you don't have strategic reasons for giving, then you're just taking a detour on the path to progress. And detours are things we mostly should avoid. Oh sure, it makes you feel good to throw a few dollars toward a worthy cause or a person in need now and then, the same way it's fun to take the long way home every once in a while. But that's not being good at being rich.

SPONTANEOUS, SPORADIC, SPARINGLY

This explains why giving is spontaneous for so many people. When your goal is to accumulate wealth and avoid losing it, you also tend to avoid giving because it feels a lot like losing something. But then you see a commercial showing a bunch of starving kids in Africa, or you pass a homeless person begging for food. Spontaneously, you react with generosity. In those occasional situations, anyone can be guilted or coerced into doing a good deed. But that's hardly a plan for keeping wealth's side effects at bay. Can you imagine taking the same approach with smallpox?

Without a plan, giving is sporadic at best. You give when you're in the Christmas spirit or when there's a food drive at the grocery store. It feels generous. And it is. But it doesn't do much to keep you from drifting toward arrogance or hoping in riches.

Without a plan, giving tends to be sparing as well. Remember, vaccinations feel counterintuitive. You don't just wake up one morning and say, "Hey, I think I'll get a shot in the arm today." Like most plans, there's plenty of built-in resistance to overcome. You'll be bombarded by impulses to hoard your money, give away less, and play it safe. Unless you're following a giving plan, you'll probably lose most of your battles against those impulses.

Being generous isn't easy. But it doesn't mean taking a vow of poverty either. It simply means following a plan to keep your giving in proportion to your income and assets.

Paul commanded us to be generous not because he wanted our money, but because he didn't want our money to have us. As we've said, there's more to generosity than simply giving something away. Just as wealth has negative side effects, *giving away wealth* has positive side effects. Generosity is the antidote for the dizzying effects of wealth.

Paul commanded us to be generous not because he wanted our money, but because he didn't want our money to have us.

Chapter 5

GREATER GAIN

*What is necessary to change a person is
to change his awareness of himself.*

Abraham Maslow

In the previous chapter, we discussed the importance of generosity. Both Paul and Jesus were uncomfortably clear on this topic. Rich people should give more than the rest of the population. Rich Christians in particular. We closed the chapter by saying that *generosity is the antidote for the dizzying effects of wealth.* And it is. Problem is, there is an antidote to extravagant generosity. And until we identify and address it, we may celebrate the notion of extravagant generosity, but we will never fully embrace it as a lifestyle. Let me explain.

To embrace the type of generosity we discussed in chapter 4 will eventually force us to say no to ourselves. Rich people don't like to be told no, even if they are the ones doing the telling. The two primary advantages of having extra money are the ability to purchase extra stuff and the luxury of securing the future by saving extra cash. The kind of generosity Jesus talks about will eventually interfere with both. There will be a conflict of wills. We will have to say no to him or no to ourselves. Did I mention that rich people don't like to be told no? Actually, nobody likes to be told no.

Whenever being told no is an issue, it is an issue surrounding an appetite. In the case of money, it's an appetite for stuff, status, or security. Truth is, if you embrace extravagant generosity, you will be forced to say no to your appetite for *more* stuff, *more* status, and *more* security. Speaking of *more*, I love what my friend Justin Grunewald says, "Appetites have only one word in their vocabularies—MORE." True, isn't it? Here's why. And this is extraordinarily important. Appetites are never fully and finally satisfied. Never. They can be temporarily satisfied. But even after the most satisfying meal imaginable, we eventually find ourselves rummaging through the pantry for a snack. Years after moving into your dream home, you find yourself driving through a new neighborhood and wondering if it's time to move.

Appetites aren't bad things. I believe God created them. I also believe sin distorted them. Appetites bring zest and passion to life. But they are terrible filters for making decisions. I don't think it is an exaggeration to say that your responses to your appetites will determine the direction and quality of your life. You've certainly seen friends and family members wreck their lives over their seeming inability to say no to themselves. So this is a big deal.

Appetites aren't bad things. I believe God created them. I also believe sin distorted them.

As you might imagine, there have been many studies centered on the role of appetites in the human experience. The people who spend their lives studying these things tell us that several changes take place in the brain when our appetites are stimulated. One of these changes is called "impact bias." Simply put, when an appetite is stimulated, the brain magnifies it out of proportion to our other appetites. Experientially, we overestimate how happy we will be if we can satisfy that particular appetite. Now. This is why smart waiters bring desserts to your table rather than simply passing out a menu. Or, in those cases when they can't bring the actual desserts, they describe them in terms that cause you to taste without seeing. Once your appetite is engaged, your brain starts lying to you. Bad brain.

Impact bias is only one of several tricks your brain plays on you when an appetite is stirred. Another is when your mind becomes so focused on one thing or bit of information that everything else is blurred or subdued in contrast. This is one reason you've driven away from a dealership convinced that you've got to have *that* car.

Yet another trick is when your brain exaggerates the consequences of not getting what your appetite desires. If you have teenagers, you've seen this in action. "Mom, if I don't get to go, I'll just DIE!" "If you make me wear this to school, I'll NEVER get a date."

So, while generosity may be the antidote for the dizzying effects of wealth, your appetite for *more* may function as an antidote against God-honoring generosity. Your appetite for more stuff, status, and security has the potential to quash your efforts to be generous. And that's a problem. A rich-person problem. If you don't address it, you may become a functioning *stuff-a-holic*, *status-a-holic*, *security-a-holic*, or some combination of the three.

So what's a girl to do?

THE GENEROUS BRAIN

We all know there is nothing new under the sun. So we shouldn't be surprised to discover that the same person who exhorted us to be rich in good deeds and generosity addresses *the* obstacle to the kind of generosity that requires us to say no to ourselves. In fact, it's in the same chapter of the same epistle. Paul writes:

> But godliness with contentment is great gain.
> *(1 Timothy 6:6)*

Contentment. There's a concept we don't hear much about. And let's be honest, isn't it *discontentment* that fuels our unnecessary, irresponsible, and, at times, harmful spending? Paul goes so far as to say that contentment is *great gain*. Translation: *Contentment* is more valuable than the things you acquired because of your *discontentment*. Looking back, we know this to be the case.

Ever regretted a large purchase? If you could go back and choose contentment with what you had over the purchase your discontentment caused you to make, wouldn't you have done it? Of course. Why? Because with hindsight you can see the *value* or the *gain* of opting for contentment. Opting for contentment would have actually made you richer. Ever wasted money? Why? I bet there was an appetite involved. Looking back, contentment would have left you richer and with one less regret. Paul knew what he was talking about. If you are truly interested in *gain*, contentment is the ticket.

Three verses later, he writes:

Those who want to get rich fall into temptation and a trap and into many foolish and harmful desires that plunge people into ruin and destruction. *(1 Timothy 6:9)*

Been there, done that? Look carefully at his words: "foolish and harmful desires." Desires. There's that appetite thing again. Then he writes one of the most famous and misquoted statements in the New Testament:

For the love of money is a root of all kinds of evil. Some people, eager for money, have wandered from the faith and pierced themselves with many griefs. *(1 Timothy 6:10)*

So to summarize Paul's observations: By refusing the gain that comes with contentment and opting instead for the gain fueled by discontentment, we run the risk of:

- Falling into temptation
- Falling into a trap
- Being controlled by harmful, habit-forming desires
- Plunging headfirst into ruin
- Plunging headfirst into destruction
- Wandering from the faith
- Piercing ourselves with many griefs

FIGHTIN' THE FIGHT

My hunch is that you know someone whose appetite-fueled discontentment drove him or her into one or more of those destinations. I bet you know someone who is headed in one of those directions at this very moment. And while it's obvious to you, she can't see it, can she? And that brings me to a question that rich people don't like to be asked. Is it possible that *you* are being lured toward one of these undesirable destinations and don't know it? Is it possible that your brain has deceived you? That your appetite is controlling you? I realize you have been blessed with an above-average IQ and are college-educated. Chances are you even have a post-graduate degree. And yes, I know you are rich. And we rich people often wrongly assume we are the smartest people in the room. Certainly too smart to be outsmarted by our own appetites! But it happens, doesn't it? It could happen to you. It could be *happening* to you. If you don't know how to harness the power of contentment, I can pretty much assure you that it *is* happening to you.

But as we've discovered, we aren't the first generation of rich Christians to fall prey to our appetites. So Paul finishes with an appeal to another set of appetites that inhabits the soul of every rich man and woman—the appetite to succeed and to win.

> But you, man of God, flee from all this, and pursue righteousness, godliness, faith, love, endurance and gentleness. Fight the good fight of the faith. *(1 Timothy 6:11–12)*

Flee. Pursue. Fight. Those are pretty strong words. To avoid being sucked into the discontentment vortex, we need to be proactive. Intentional. Aggressive. Generosity doesn't come naturally. Saying no to ourselves is not intuitive. Apparently, the more we have, the more we'll be controlled by our insatiable appetites for more. Which doesn't really make sense. It seems like the more we have, the less we would want. Ahhh, but that's not the way of appetites.

Case in point ... several years ago Sandra and I were doing a financial study with the small group that meets in our home. All seven couples were in their mid-to-late forties. We all had kids ranging in age from middle school to high school. Part of our homework one week was to sit down as a couple and identify the season in our marriage when we were most content. Then we would report our findings the next time we met. What about you? At what stage of life were you most content with what you had?

At what stage of life were you most content with what you had?

Everyone in our group came to the same conclusion. We all agreed that we experienced the most contentment in the early years of marriage when we had significantly less. Which doesn't make a bit of sense, does it? How could we have more contentment and less stuff? Doesn't the acquisition of stuff scratch the discontentment itch? Apparently not. Actually, the opposite is true. Thus, our conclusion. And chances are you came to the same conclusion regarding your own sense of contentment.

But why is that? How can less stuff result in greater contentment? The answer is found in one final observation regarding the nature of appetites: If you feed an appetite, it grows. Satisfying an appetite does not diminish it. It expands it. To diminish an appetite, you have to starve it. So, in the early days of marriage, when none of us in our group had a lot of extra money to do extra things, we didn't do extra things. And we were content. We were forced to starve that appetite. But once our incomes and our purchasing power began to increase, we started feeding that ugly beast. In doing so, we gave up a slice of contentment. And so it goes.

Paul understood this. In fact, he took this principle to a logical but uncomfortable extreme. He writes:

> For we brought nothing into the world, and we can take
> nothing out of it. But if we have food and clothing, we
> will be content with that. *(1 Timothy 6:7–8)*

Food and clothing. No Internet. But imagine how much money you would save ... how much money you could give ... if you went for a whole year content to provide yourself with the minimal level of food, shelter, and clothing. I'm not suggesting it. I would be a hypocrite if I did. But it's impossible to miss his point. If Paul contented himself with the minimum, that was certainly great gain for him and for those to whom he chose to give his extra.

Fighting for, pursuing, and embracing contentment always results in gain. Every time. At multiple levels. And that brings us to a most important question. A question that this entire chapter has been building toward. A question I'll ask three different ways for maximum effect!

> How does one find contentment in a media-saturated cul-
> ture built on an advertisement-driven economy?

How do you say "enough" in a world that has fine-tuned its messaging so as to make you continually dissatisfied with everything you currently own?

How can we rich people, the ones with extra money, find the will power to say no when, technically, we can afford to say yes?

The answer is found in a single word. A word that works for us or against us. If you are carrying debt on something you wished you had never purchased, then you know all about this word and the power it wields. As we close this chapter, I'm going to teach you how to leverage this word so it will work in your favor. I'm convinced this single term holds the key to disarming discontentment.

The word is: *awareness*. Awareness fuels discontentment. But awareness can be used to tether and tame it as well.

AWARENESS MANAGEMENT

We are all aware of the power of awareness. This is not an unfamiliar dynamic. How many times have you gone to the store for a single item, and by the time you reached the checkout, your cart was full? More times than you can remember. While cruising the aisles, you see something you didn't even know existed, and in less time than it takes to pick it up off the shelf, you convince yourself this is something you actually *need*. Not simply *want*. Our brains skip right over want and go directly to need. That's amazing, isn't it? Actually, it's scary. Seeing is needing. That's the power of awareness.

Awareness is a critical concept in sales and marketing. Without it, and the discontentment it enflames, consumers don't buy as much. Apart from a daily dose of discontentment, we'd be perfectly happy with the stuff we already own. That's why product manufacturers and their advertising agencies keep such close track of brand *awareness*. They run expensive commercials and conduct expensive research to manage our awareness of their products. The higher the awareness, the stronger the discontentment, and the better the sales. But it wasn't always this way.

Years ago, discontentment didn't play such a big role in purchases. Prior to today's sophisticated marketing machines, people bought based on *need*. Imagine such a thing. They would *replace* something when it broke. How passé. Today, we don't replace things when they break. We replace things when the newer model of the thing we already own becomes available. We *upgrade*. And *when* do we upgrade? When we become *aware* that the upgrade is available. Granted, we may wait until we *see* somebody else using his upgraded device, driving her upgraded car, cooking on his upgraded cooktop, or rockin' her upgraded wardrobe. But once we are aware that the products are out there, we start scheming. (I mean planning.) Once we become aware of what we don't have, we become hopelessly discontented. Now, as I mentioned earlier, this can work *for* you as well as against you. But it's going to take some effort. As Paul said, you are going to have to fight for it.

Perhaps a story will help.

PLAYING DRESS-UP

In December 2008, I received an invitation from the White House to participate in the National Prayer Service, an event that takes place at the Washington National Cathedral the morning following the inauguration. It was an honor to be asked and I accepted immediately. In addition to the President and his family, the Cabinet, members of Congress, Supreme Court justices, and several hundred invited guests would attend.

When I shared the news with Sandra, one of her first remarks was, "What will I wear?" Like all of the invited religious leaders, we were instructed to dress according to our faith tradition. Sandra assured me that I would not be dressed according to *my* faith tradition. And she was not about to show up dressed according to hers. We are very casual people. At the time, I owned one outdated suit. Sandra's closet was full of jeans, jackets, and blouses. So we had some shopping to do.

Shopping for me was easy. I needed a new blue suit and a tie. For Sandra, it was not that easy. So one Thursday morning she embarked on a search to find something suitable to wear to our big event. Late in the afternoon I called her to see how it was going.

"I found the perfect outfit!" she announced. But I sensed something mischievous in her tone. "It's a beautiful suit, the fabric is gorgeous, and it looks incredible." Long pause.

"Where are you?" I asked. When she told me, I knew what all the mystery was about. She was in the most exclusive department store in Atlanta. A place we never shop.

She laughed and said, "And it's only $3,000! Not including blouse or shoes, of course."

Two simultaneous thoughts ran through my head in that moment. First thought: *How can a jacket and skirt cost $3,000?* Had it been worn by Jacqueline Kennedy at her husband's inauguration? Second thought: *If she really wants it, she certainly deserves it, and I'll find a way to get it. And then . . . eBay.* Think about it. We could advertise that it was worn only once. And what a *once* it was! Sandra is the most content, nonmaterialistic woman I know. But I also knew that she wanted to be dressed appropriately for our date at the National Cathedral.

Before I could express either of these fleeting thoughts, she burst out laughing. "Don't worry. I'm not about to spend $3,000 on an outfit." But it was what she said next that made our conversation memorable. Not only does it illustrate the positive power of awareness, but it also shows that leveraging awareness in this way requires a bit of intentionality.

"When I looked at that price tag, all I could see were the precious faces of those orphans at New Hope Homes in Kigali, Rwanda. And I thought, *Imagine what $3,000 would do for them.*" I get misty-eyed every time I think about that conversation.

Earlier that year, our family hosted five other families on a trip to Rwanda and Tanzania to tour several Compassion International sites. The goal of the trip was to expose these families to the work of Compassion in hopes that they would become donors. There's that awareness thing again, huh? Hearing about what an organization such as Compassion does is one thing. Seeing it, smelling it, touring it is something altogether different. During our time in Kigali, we visited a family we had met a few years earlier in Nairobi. In addition to their role with Compassion, they were building group homes for children who had no living family members. They called their project "New Hope Homes." One hundred American dollars goes a long way in an environment like that. Three thousand American dollars was almost enough to fund an entire two-bedroom addition to their current building. Knowing that, being *aware* of that, put a $3,000 suit that Sandra might wear three or four times over the course of her life in an entirely new light.

Awareness is a powerful thing. If awareness can curb a woman's appetite for *the perfect* outfit, what can't it do? Awareness has the potential to drive your discontentment in one of two directions. It can fuel appetites that will never be satisfied. Or it can propel you toward unprecedented generosity, while curbing your appetite to spend. In the end, Sandra purchased a beautiful outfit from a local department store. Total bill: $290 plus shoes. She looked so stunning that a former President went out of his way to walk over and shake her hand. No lie. She's gonna kill me for telling you that.

TURNABOUT IS FAIR PLAY

If you are going to be good at being rich, then you must begin *cultivating awareness* of things that really matter. Opportunities that make a real difference in the world.

Things that matter to our heavenly Father. It takes no dis-cipline or effort on our parts to be made aware of what we don't have but could have. Culture will take care of that. But it takes initiative to become and remain aware of what other people don't have but should have. We will have to make a concerted effort to keep the needs of others in the forefront of our thinking. Not for guilt's sake, but for the sake of being good stewards of the resources we have been privileged to manage.

Every spending and saving decision we make is made within a framework of awareness. To be good at being rich, we must broaden that framework. We must make it a habit to see beyond our neighborhoods, our schools, and our current geographical frames of reference. If we don't, eventually our awareness will be limited to our individual experiences. And while we may remain rich, we will no longer be rich in good deeds. We will no longer feel compelled to share. *Seeing* will become *needing* because we will have lost our awareness of what it means to be in need.

Isn't it strange? You miss money you misspend. You miss money you waste or poorly invest. But you never miss money given to meet a need in someone's life. Put another way, we become discontented with ourselves when we mishandle our money, but we find contentment through responsible gener-osity. As Paul says, it is a contentment that brings great gain.

You never miss money given to meet a need in someone's life.

There are many ways to immerse yourself in environments that will heighten your awareness of the things that matter most to God. You don't have to leave the country. Awareness is one of the reasons we encourage people in our churches to volunteer at the organizations we fund through our *Be Rich* campaign. Hearing about people in need heightens awareness. But *serving* people in need takes awareness to an even greater level. Staring into the eyes of a child who won't get anything for Christmas apart from our generosity helps curb our appetites for things we are tempted to talk ourselves into *needing*. Again, awareness is a powerful thing.

But increasing our awareness of what others need is only one way to leverage the power of awareness. A second approach involves disconnecting or *uncoupling* ourselves from the various awareness pipelines to which we are connected. For example, stay out of the mall! Cancel a magazine subscription or two. Quit receiving that electronics catalog. Skip the home show, the boat show, and the gun-and-knife show this year. Stop unnecessarily exposing yourself to environments that make you discontent with what you have. Look for ways to become less aware of what you don't have and don't need. By doing so, you leverage the power of awareness in your favor. You make it easier to say no to you and yes to those who could benefit from your generosity.

Generosity *is*, in fact, the antidote for the dizzying effects of wealth. But discontentment—fueled by our insatiable appetites for more—has the power to dilute our generosity. Awareness, however, when leveraged correctly, has the power to tame and redirect our discontentment. In this way, awareness is the antidote to discontentment. Now that you're aware, I suggest you get busy leveraging it for good.

That's how to *be rich*.

Chapter 6

OWNERSHIP MYTH

What I possess, God owns.

Howard Dayton

*If one first gives himself to the Lord,
all other giving is easy.*

John S. Bonnell

So far we've explored how to be good at being rich from several different angles. We've seen that if you don't even know *when* you're rich, it's difficult to be good at *being* rich. We looked at several things Paul commanded rich people to do in order to be good at it. We learned about the danger of assuming that all of our possessions are intended for our own consumption. And we saw how generosity is the antidote for the negative side effects of wealth.

Those are great principles for everyone who hopes to be rich someday. But if you really want to be good at being rich, there's one more thing you should know. In fact, you can practice everything else we've talked about, but without this next principle, avoiding the side effects of wealth will be a constant struggle. It's an idea presented in the Old Testament and mirrored in the New Testament. If you're one of those people who likes to cut right to the core issue at hand, then you'll probably want to start with this principle. Because once a person gets it right here, all the other aspects of being good at being rich come easy.

The principle simply says, "Your success with regard to wealth is determined by your objective with regard to wealth." In other words, when you reduce this whole topic down to its minimum complexity, your ability to be a good rich person is ultimately a function of the core objective you embrace when it comes to riches. There are many objectives a person might have when it comes to money. And each one has a predetermined outcome in terms of being able to look back on your life and celebrate that you were good at being rich.

For some people, their basic objective for money is to provide for their families. And that's a great goal. But if that's your only objective for money, you won't necessarily be good at being rich. A lot of wealthy people that take great care of their families still struggle to give generously.

For other people, the goal is to make as much money as they can. And they're good at it. But making money doesn't make you good at managing money, does it? So there has to be something more.

Another objective might be to save as much as possible. You measure every opportunity by how it enables you to grow your savings account. That's certainly a great objective. Saving is incredibly important. But that won't guarantee that you'll look back on your life one day and declare that you were good at being rich.

For still other people, their objective is to spend money well. I don't mean they're frivolous and careless. They just see money as a tool to accomplish other things. What good does it do for you to die with a large bank account, only to have it divided among your survivors? So they spend wisely, and they spend frequently, and that's how they measure their progress. But you can spot the holes in that plan right away. You can end up neglecting a lot of other important things you need to accomplish in order to be good at being rich.

While each of those goals has merit, I want to introduce you to the one objective that pulls all others into balance, the one thing that can be considered true north on your compass when it comes to finances. Serve this objective faithfully, and everything else will fall into place. Achieve it, and you will be good at being rich. Best of all, it provides a clear grid system for guiding every financial decision you'll make in life. When it comes to why you have money in the first place, and what to do with it while you do, this principle holds the key to a perspective that will lead to good decisions and good management of your money.

WHEN KINGS BOW DOWN

Three thousand years ago, David was the king of Israel. Reaching the throne was not exactly smooth sailing for him. There were wars, scandals, and betrayals—some of the most dramatic stories in recorded history. For years, David had led his people on a nomadic journey to make God's chosen people a nation. They lived in tents and even carried a portable version of God's house called the tabernacle, which contained the ark of the covenant.

Eventually, though, David reached a point in his life when he'd arrived. All of his enemies had been defeated. All the battles had been won. Israel was the reigning superpower of the time, and there was peace in the land. In short, he was rich. One day it dawned on him how blessed he was. He lived in an incredible palace in an incredible kingdom at an amazing time in history.

David's situation is not unlike yours and mine today. We live in the richest country during the richest time in history. If he could see us now, David would say we live like kings every day. And as he looked around him on this particular day, it evoked within him a response that gives us a model of how we should view our own situations.

David had always seen God's hand in everything. God was present in every giant David faced, every battle he fought, and every victory he won. In fact, David wrote numerous psalms to praise God for being the provider of all he received. But now, as he looked out from his palatial home, he couldn't help noticing that God had only a temporary home. The tabernacle was nothing more than a tent. So David resolved in his heart to build a permanent home for God—a temple. And David set out to begin designing the architecture and raising the money for what would eventually become known as Solomon's Temple, one of the seven wonders of the ancient world. David allocated gold and silver from Israel's national treasury to pay for construction. He even donated a large portion of his own money for the project. Some scholars put David's personal contribution at about $14 billion.

When David called the Israelites together in Jerusalem to announce the plan to build the temple, the people were excited. Money started pouring in. They were still in touch with all God had done to bring them to this place of blessing. And their participation was heartfelt.

In the midst of all this euphoria, David prayed a prayer

that gives us insight into his heart and perspective regarding life, God, and the purpose of money. Through this prayer, we discover the one primary objective that should guide the way we think about and handle our money. This mindset is the key to being good at being rich. It begins like this:

> Praise be to you, LORD, the God of our father Israel, from everlasting to everlasting. Yours, LORD, is the greatness and the power and the glory and the majesty and the splendor. *(1 Chronicles 29:10–11a)*

In essence, David was looking back over all that God had taken the Israelites through, and he concluded, "God, this is all about you." Here's the king of the greatest superpower on earth, and he's publicly bowing down before God, whom he considers to be the King of kings. And that includes King David. He continued:

> For everything in heaven and earth is yours. Yours, LORD, is the kingdom; you are exalted as head over all. *(1 Chronicles 29:11b)*

As far as David was concerned, everything belonged to God. That included all the gold and silver from the treasury and all the money from the people. All of it belonged to God anyway. They were just moving God's money from one place to the next in order to build a permanent home for the ark of the covenant. Next, he said:

> Wealth and honor come from you; you are the ruler of all things. In your hands are strength and power to exalt and give strength to all. *(1 Chronicles 29:12)*

From David's perspective, not only did God own all material things, but he was also the source of the things money can't buy—things like honor and power and strength. David's comment was meant to describe everything a person enjoys in life, as well as everything that enables our accomplishments. And it wasn't just true for David, but for all the people throughout the nation and around the world. No matter who held what, it ultimately belonged to God.

This statement must have been astounding to some of David's onlookers. Many had seen how hard David had worked to become king. They had witnessed his cunning in battle. They'd seen his wisdom as a leader. They'd watched him make sacrifices for the good of the nation. But now David was openly professing to his people that it was God who enabled those things. He couldn't begin to take credit for the things he had achieved.

In short, David was declaring that everything belongs to God, everything comes from God, and everything is dispensed by God. He concluded with this:

> Now, our God, we give you thanks, and praise your glorious name. But who am I, and who are my people, that we should be able to give as generously as this? Everything comes from you, and we have given you only what comes from your hand. *(1 Chronicles 29:13–14)*

Wow. What a perspective! You don't see many rich people these days responding like that, do you? David even considered himself unworthy of the opportunity to be generous. This mindset is just the opposite of what many rich

Americans convey today. In contrast, they seem to say, "This is mine. I worked hard for this, and I'm entitled to do whatever I want with it." Here in the land of opportunity, it's generally perceived that success is the by-product of hard work. And while that may be true in many cases, it's God who gives us both the ability and the opportunity to work hard. Once again, everything comes from him.

So if everything belongs to God, comes from God, and is dispensed by God, what should be the one thing that governs our approach to money? How do you summarize David's mindset about money? If you want to replicate his perspective in your own life, what should your main objective be?

As I think about that prayer, two words come to mind: *Honor God.* Those two words encapsulate all the things David declared about his riches. If you were to pursue only one goal for everything you possess, this should be it. Honor God. Serve that single objective and everything else automatically falls into place.

If you were to pursue only one goal for everything you possess, this should be it. Honor God.

THE GIVING MYTH

If you've been around the church world for any length of time, it's not easy to get your head around what David's really saying here. You see, David says *everything* belongs to

God—not just the percentage we put in the offering plate. I was taught from an early age to give God 10 percent of everything. That meant if I got a dollar, I put ten cents in the offering plate. If I got ten dollars, one of them went to the work of the church. And so on. I'm very thankful that I was raised to practice that core value.

But I have to admit, that routine by itself doesn't quite engender the mindset that David expressed in his prayer. Even if you give 10 percent faithfully, it doesn't mean you'll come away with the right perspective about the other 90 percent. In fact, over time you can become a little possessive about it. *As long as I give God his cut, I'm free to do whatever I want with the other 90 percent. God, here's yours. Now I'm taking the rest for me.* Somehow, even tithing can become a task we check off our lists before moving on to something else. *I gave my 10 percent. The rest is mine to do with whatever I want.* That doesn't sound much like what David believed, does it?

It was always easy for me to give God ten cents out of a dollar or ten dollars out of a hundred. I also remember getting a check for a thousand dollars and having no hesitation about giving God his hundred. But I'll be honest, when it got much bigger than that, a little alarm would start to go off inside. If you get a check for ten thousand dollars, are you really going to write a check for a thousand dollars? That's a lot of money. And even if it's only for a split second, you can almost feel irresponsible about giving away that much money.

If you've ever experienced that feeling, you know what I'm talking about. And there's a simple explanation for it. Whenever we sense that little hesitation, it's because we've started to view our money as *our* money. Unlike David, we don't really think of it as being God's. In those moments, we're not completely in touch with the fact that everything belongs to him, comes from him, and is dispensed by him. In a way, we're buying into the myth that we own it, and we're giving it to God.

I call it a myth because, as David pointed out, *who am I that I should be able to give as generously as this?* God owns it all anyway. So I'm really just "giving" him what already belongs to him. Whenever I give God something, it's really just symbolic. The idea that we ever "give" God anything is really just a myth.

The idea that we ever "give" God anything is really just a myth.

As David's prayer suggests, it's not about *giving*, it's about *living*. And the same theme is found throughout Scripture. We are to honor God not with a percentage, but with all that we possess. It's not 10 percent. It's 100 percent.

When you view your possessions that way, it changes everything.

ON LOAN

A few years ago, the High Museum of Art in Atlanta signed an agreement with the Louvre in Paris in which priceless art from Europe would come to Atlanta "on loan." The collection included one-of-a-kind masterpieces from a span of 4,000 years. There were rare works by Raphael, Rembrandt, and Michelangelo. It was incredible. According to the agreement, everything still belonged to the Louvre. It was just being entrusted to the care of their American counterparts.

So here's a question: What percentage of that art collection did the Louvre expect the Americans to take care of? Do you think they'd have been satisfied if we sent 10 percent of it back with a note explaining that we used the other canvases to patch a leak in the roof? Not likely. World wars have been started over less. Of course, both parties understood that every irreplaceable piece would be cared for with absolute vigilance. Not even a fingerprint would be permitted.

The governing principle behind that art exchange was *ownership*. The Louvre owned it all. And, therefore, everybody understood the responsibility of handling it properly. In essence, the Americans were bound to honor the expectations of the owners. Because that's what you do when you handle other people's stuff.

Is that how you view your stuff? Not just your money, but things like honor, strength, and opportunity too? Again, according to David, everything that's "yours" belongs to God, comes from God, and is dispensed by God. And here's the clincher. God sees things that way too. It's all his. It's just on loan to you.

That being the case, what would it look like for you to honor God with *all* of your stuff?

Now I have to ask you: Does that question give you butterflies in your stomach? Are you getting images of being called to the mission field, taking a vow of poverty, and living in squalor the rest of your life? Because if the thought of turning everything over to God makes you a little nervous, you're not alone. But here's what I want you to remember. God doesn't want to take your money; he just doesn't want your money to take you.

First of all, he doesn't need your permission to take your stuff. It's already his anyway. And second, God is a giver, not a taker. He didn't send his Son, Jesus, to collect from everyone who owed him. He sent Jesus to *give* his life for you. And by calling you to acknowledge him as the owner of your stuff, he wants to give you something yet again. He wants to give you the freedom and peace that come with letting go. Did you know that the more you hold on to what you possess, the less peace you have?

God is a giver, not a taker. He sent Jesus to *give* his life for you.

So let me ask you again: What would it look like for you to honor God with *all* of your stuff? For starters, are you already honoring him with the first 10 percent? If you're not there yet, that's a great place to begin. If you are, do you need to take it up a notch in the area of giving? Maybe bump it up a percentage or two?

Or perhaps honoring God would mean stepping up in the area of providing for your family. For some people, honoring God means saving more, spending less, or liquidating that cabinet full of collectibles. I don't know where this will land for you. But if you ask God, he will show you how to honor him with everything you have. Not just with a percentage of it, but with all of it.

THIS PRESENT AGE

David knew something else about honoring God with his stuff. He knew that his days were numbered. I don't mean that he was about to die. But in the grand scheme of life, David had a limited amount of time with which to honor God. We all do. And David knew that whatever he did in this life was somehow connected to life in eternity.

In fact, if you recall Paul's instructions to Timothy, he makes reference to this very same idea. He said:

> Command those who are rich in this present world ...
> *(1 Timothy 6:17)*

Did you catch that? *In this present world*? Why would Paul word it that way? Is there a non-present world? Like a future world? In this statement, the apostle Paul tips his hand to the fact that he believes there is more to this life than this life. He believes there is something beyond this life. And he's not alone. Ninety-seven percent of Americans believe there is something beyond this life. There's another world *besides* this present world. And even if someone's rich in this world, it won't last forever. Another world is coming right after it. So rather than carry on like nothing will ever change, rich people need to honor God with their stuff now.

Because not only are they guarding against the side effects of wealth here, they're actually laying up treasure in heaven for an age that is yet to come.

There are many theories to describe exactly what that looks like, and I certainly won't attempt to explain heaven or the afterlife here. But you can be sure of this: Jesus talked about this concept throughout the Gospels, so there's little doubt that the degree to which we honor God during this age will impact our experience in the age to come.

Paul instructs Timothy to tell rich people that they get one opportunity to do good in such a way that they will impact their standing in the age to come. Don't miss the opportunity.

When Jesus talked about it, he was very clear. He asked the question, "What good is it for someone to gain the whole world, yet forfeit their soul?" (Mark 8:36). In essence, he implored his followers to view wealth through the lens of eternity. That's how David viewed it. And when we do the same, we lose our grip on wealth, and wealth loses its grip on us.

Chapter 7

IT CAN HAPPEN AGAIN

*Kindness is the language which the
deaf can hear and the blind can see.*

Mark Twain

O ne of the most compelling arguments for the Christian faith is the simple fact that it survived. The odds against it were incredible. If you look at the typical building blocks that result in the longevity of a movement, Christianity has had none of them. The longest-enduring movements throughout history were political interests backed by military might or social efforts fueled by the power of the people. Some movements had superior weapons; others had powerful unions. Even the peaceful protests that we know of succeeded because they appealed to the sympathies of the masses and resulted in political power.

First-century Christians weren't organized, had no buildings, and weren't recognized by the government. In everyday society, they were basically considered a cult. For nearly three centuries, they remained utterly powerless—ostracized socially, persecuted politically, and tortured physically. And yet somehow their movement continued to grow.

How do you explain that?

Over the years, a number of historians have explored this phenomenon in detail. People such as Rodney Stark, Paul Johnson, and Alvin Schmidt have dedicated much of their careers to understanding how Christianity could not only survive but actually thrive. Their conclusion is nothing short of remarkable.

While Christianity had none of the conventional strengths required to start a movement, its appeal and influence can be traced to an unexpected source: generosity.

The hallmark of Christians in the first century was not their wealth. They had none. It was not their theology either. Their beliefs were so odd, religious people couldn't understand them. What gave them leverage was their inexplicable compassion and generosity. They had little, but they gave. They received little compassion, but they were willing to extend what they had to other people. They were impossible to ignore.

The hallmark of Christians in the first century was not their wealth. They had none. It was not their theology either.

AN EYE FOR AN EYE

I can't overemphasize what a monumental shift this was for the people of Jesus' time. Throughout the Greek and Roman eras, the guiding principle for how to treat other people was very different from what we know today. The rule of thumb for things like courtesy, etiquette, and decency was summed up in the Latin word *liberalitas*. The word basically means that you give in order to get something in return. It's how the system works. Everybody looks out for one another. You scratch my back; I'll scratch yours.

In fact, the word *liberalitas* can still be found on much of the coinage from that era. Roman emperors printed their own coinage. There was even a custom in which the emperor would go through the streets of the main city and throw handfuls of coins into the crowd to cultivate loyalty. In essence, it meant that he was giving to the people so that if he were ever in need, they'd be ready to give back to him. Can't you just see the parade-like atmosphere? The crowd is chanting, *"Liberalitas! Liberalitas!"* while being showered with coins bearing that word.

As you can imagine, in a *liberalitas* economy, there wasn't much use for someone who couldn't pay you back. Why would you waste good deeds on someone who couldn't return the favor? The whole idea of generosity in that culture was *find someone who can do something for you and do something for him first.* Because then he'll owe you.

This can be really hard for us to understand today. We're surrounded by examples of sacrifice. It's part of our culture. It's the theme of our movies. It's the mantra of our public officials. And it's the call of duty for our military men and women. Not everybody does it. But it's the benchmark against which we measure things such as honor, integrity, and faithfulness. Whenever someone sacrifices something, expecting nothing in return, we recognize it and respect it. It inspires us.

But during the first century, that legacy didn't exist. The only reason to give liberally was in order to receive liberally sometime in the future. Even in Jewish culture, there was a tendency to give to someone based on his or her ability to return the favor. Generosity was all about doing for others so others could do for you. Consequently, the people who had the most also received the most. And the people who had nothing? They got nothing.

Essentially, it was an economy based on reciprocity. As long as you had some kind of wealth or power or leverage, you had the hope of receiving the same from others.

This explains why the situation was so desperate for widows and orphans. They were penniless and powerless. There was absolutely no incentive for helping them. You were almost guaranteed not to get anything in return. It was commonly understood that helping a widow or an orphan was a total waste of time and/or money. You'd never see anything from it. So nobody did it. And nobody would shame you for taking that position.

Then along came Jesus.

A DEED FOR A NEED

Jesus walked right into the middle of that culture and announced that his kingdom would be different. His would be based on the kindness economy. In Jesus' kingdom, people would give and not expect to be repaid. In Jesus' kingdom, people would lend knowing they might never get it back. In Jesus' kingdom, you would do for others what they couldn't do for you in return. He even said to love your enemies! Do good to them. You know *they're* not going to pay you back. When you show kindness like that, he says, then your reward will be great. Then you will be children of the Most High. After all, God is kind to the ungrateful and the wicked. And as his representatives throughout the world, we should reflect his kind of generosity—the kind that expects nothing in return.

Jesus challenged his hearers with provocative questions. He observed that if you love those who love you, it's really no credit to you. After all, even sinners can love those who treat them well. The same is true for good deeds. Even sinners will do good when they get something in return. That's just *liberalitas*. Jesus' style of generosity was different.

Jesus' style of generosity was different.

In essence, Jesus was shifting the world's concept of love. He invented a story about a Samaritan man who, because of his race, would have been considered contemptible by Jesus' listeners. The Samaritan stopped to help a non-Samaritan man who had been beaten and robbed. Under normal circumstances, these two would have had nothing to do with each other. They were culturally incompatible. But Jesus picked these characters on purpose. And as he told the story, the audience leaned in to hear what would happen. Would a Samaritan really help a non-Samaritan? Would the non-Samaritan even accept the Samaritan's help? Jesus was making a point: *That's what it means to be a neighbor.*

He didn't stop there. One night he gathered his closest

followers for a final meal together. He was their leader. He was not only the most powerful person in the room, but he was the head of a growing movement. What's more, he stood up and announced that he'd been given complete authority over the entire world. Then, rather than commanding them to bow at his feet or to humble themselves before him, he did something completely unexpected. He got down on the floor and washed everyone's feet. And as he did, he explained that the rules were going to be different in his kingdom. Whenever people were in positions of power, authority, or influence, they were not to use such positions for themselves. Instead, they were to leverage them for the good of those who had less power, authority, and influence. And after he washed their feet, he told them to do the same for others.

For the next three hundred years, they did just that. They went out into the world with a brand of generosity the world had never seen. They gave to those who could never return the favor. They did good deeds that would never be reciprocated. And as they did, the world was watching. They knew that a whole new kind of love had somehow come to the planet. And they couldn't help but be drawn to it.

A LEGACY OF GENEROSITY

Generosity was nothing short of the hallmark of the first-century church. It was all they had. And it proved to be more influential than any amount of money or political sway. As time went on, several plagues ripped through the cities of that region. Each time, the people would flee to the country to escape death. Whenever they did, the sick were left with no one to care for them. However, historians tell us, the Christians didn't flee. Instead, they risked their own health to stay and meet the needs of the ones who couldn't help themselves. Many of these Christians died in the process. But they weren't afraid of death. As they nursed the sick back to health, word of their generosity spread like wildfire.

The entire perspective of the Christians stood in stark contrast to the pagans around them. The pagan priests were the first to leave town in those situations. They were some of the wealthiest people around, and they had a lot to lose. Not to mention the fact that they were afraid of death. So they thought nothing of leaving their sick loved ones behind in order to save themselves. Meanwhile, the Christians would even take care of the pagans. And as the pagans' health returned, they often abandoned their idolatrous ways and turned to Christianity. Not because of theology. Not because of a miracle. But because of the generosity and compassion of the Christians in their communities.

One such story that survived antiquity records the saga of a man named Pachomius. He was twenty years old when the Romans took over the town of Thebes, where he lived. Pachomius's parents were both pagans, and he considered that to be his lot in life as well. But when the Romans came to town, the course of his life was changed forever.

When the Roman Empire took over a community, they collected all the young men and drafted them into the Roman army. And because the Roman generals knew these men would escape if possible, they locked them in prison until they could be carted off and trained to serve. While Pachomius was in prison, a famine ravaged the area. Everyone in the prison began to starve. But as Pachomius documents, strangers began to show up at night and slip food between the bars. Night after night, the mysterious people came back. And each time they did, the prisoners inhaled the morsels without asking questions. As a result, Pachomius and his friends survived the horrible famine.

When it was over, Pachomius began to ask questions. *Who were those people? Where did they come from? And most of all, why in the world were they feeding us?* The answer bewildered him. The strangers were members of the group known as Christians, Galileans, or followers of The Way.

When Pachomius completed his obligations to the Roman infantry, he immediately sought out the Christians. From them he learned about Jesus, the resurrection, and the people who now carried out his legacy. Pachomius became a Christian and eventually was a great leader in the early church. He was later dubbed Saint Pachomius in recognition of his devotion to the movement. And it was all because of the extraordinary generosity that captured his heart.

Everywhere Christians went, they were known for their generosity. And their influence began to reshape the Roman Empire. Eventually, Emperor Julian made a push to bring back paganism. But it was the generosity of Christians that foiled his efforts. He wrote, "The impious Galileans [followers of Jesus] support not only their own poor but ours as well." Basically, he couldn't galvanize support because the Christians continued to do more for the pagans than the pagan leaders did. Not because they'd get something in return. But because that's what God's love is all about.

This version of no-strings-attached generosity was so extraordinarily powerful that it was one of the primary reasons Christianity survived the first century.

A FUTURE SO RICH

Generosity changed the world once. What would happen if the church became known for inexplicable generosity once again?

I have the incredible privilege of exploring that question with one of the most generous groups of Christians on the planet. The generosity poured out by the members of our churches continues to overflow our community and extend around the world. They embody the brand of generosity we're called to extend to others. Not just for each other, but for people living in remote parts of the world who can never pay us back.

In normal circles, these aren't people who stand out for their wealth either. They face financial uncertainty. They have economic challenges and setbacks. But despite it all, they recognize that by global standards, they're already rich.

Generosity continues to capture the attention of people from all over the world. To this day, it's a reflection of the love Jesus demonstrated. It sends a message to the world that God so loved that he gave—and there were no strings attached. The best ministry we can offer on God's behalf isn't to explain our theology. It's to extend our generosity. Because that's what our heavenly Father did for us. And that's what he's asked us to do as well.

CONCLUSION

During our time together, I hope you've made two life-style-altering discoveries. First, I hope you realize how well off you are. Odds are, you're rich. Yes, there are people who are rich-er. But let's face it, there's always an *"er"*—smart-*er*, tall-*er*, fast-*er*. Don't let that take away from the fact that you are richer than a large percentage of the people in the world. But remember, that's not something to feel guilty about. It's something to wake up every day and be grateful for. Besides, it's not yours anyway. You are a steward. A manager. Money managers don't feel guilty; they feel responsible. And that brings me to the second discovery. I hope you've discovered how to be rich.

Specifically, I hope you've learned a thing or two about how to be *good* at being rich. I hope you will never again place your hope in riches, but in him who richly provides. I pray your hope will never migrate but will instead stay centered on the only dependable Source of hope.

I hope that from this day forward you will leverage the awareness principle in order to keep your appetite for stuff in check. Remember that just because you can afford something doesn't mean you should buy it. As someone intent on being good at being rich, be intentional about exposing yourself to what God is up to in the world, along with the plight of those who lack your resources and opportunities.

On the practical side of the ledger sheet, I hope you will carve out some time to create a giving strategy. Soon. Like, as soon as you finish the book. You plan every other part of your life; why not plan your generosity? If you don't, you already know what will happen. You'll give like the average person. Do you really want to be an average giver? Do you want to be an average anything? Didn't think so. Besides, you're rich. You should give like a rich person. To do that, you need a plan. A plan that stretches you out of your comfort zone. A plan that demonstrates that your hope is not in your ability to hoard.

I hope you start giving like a rich person. That you will choose a percentage and give it first. And then as God continues to bless you with more, that you would increase the percentage. The apostle Paul summed it up best. So as we close our time together, allow me to take his powerful admonition and personalize it for all of us rich folks:

> If you are rich in this life, don't be arrogant and please don't place your hope in wealth. It's so uncertain. Instead, place your hope in God who richly provides you with

everything for your enjoyment. Do good! Be rich in good
deeds! Be generous and willing to share. When you do, you
lay up a treasure for yourself that serves as a firm foundation in the coming age. And that's not all. Selfless generosity allows you to take hold of life as it was meant to be lived.

And that's *how to be rich*!

SMALL GROUP VIDEO DISCUSSION GUIDE

HOW TO USE THE GUIDE

This discussion guide was developed for use with the *How to Be Rich* four-session video, which complements and expands the material in this book. Ideally, those leading a group discussion on *How to Be Rich* should preview each video session and read through the accompanying portion of the discussion guide before the group meets. While the material in the discussion guide is intended for use with the video, some of the discussion questions will also reflect content that is used in the book.

The four video sessions cover the overarching themes of the book. However, it is strongly recommended that you and your group view Session 1 before you begin reading the book, as Andy Stanley presents an excellent overview of *How to Be Rich* that will make your book reading and small group experience even more rewarding.

The four sessions are:

1. Congratulations
2. Side Effects
3. Dollar Cost Living
4. Diversify

FORMAT OF THE GUIDE

• **Introduction and Opening Question**—Each session features a short introduction to establish the theme. If your group wants to open with a question that serves as a discussion starter or icebreaker, please make use of this question.

• **Video Viewing**—The video clip for each session is approximately 15–20 minutes.

• **Video Discussion**—These questions are designed to follow Andy's video teaching and engage the group in discussion around the content they just watched. Some of the questions focus on Bible passages used in the video and tie in with the theme of the session.

• **Moving Forward**—This challenge helps group members consider how they might put what they learned into action.

• **Between Sessions**—Each session concludes with a key Bible passage to memorize as well as recommended reading from the book in preparation for the next meeting.

SESSION 1: CONGRATULATIONS

INTRODUCTION

Have you ever stopped to think, *How much money does it take to be R-I-C-H?* Rich always seems to be the other person. Most people think that anyone who has at least twice the wealth that they have is rich. Which means, of course, that nobody's rich, but everybody knows someone who is.

In this study, we will look at some significant words from the apostle Paul in 1 Timothy 6. In verse 17 of that chapter, Paul says, "Command those who are rich in this present world ..." So, who *are* the rich? Might Paul's words written so long ago be directed to us today?

When you hear the word "rich," what are the first things that come to your mind?

VIDEO VIEWING AND NOTES

Watch the Session 1 video, "Congratulations," together as a group and note anything that impacts you.

VIDEO DISCUSSION

1. When Andy says "if you make $48,000 or more a year, you are in the top 1 percent of wage earners in the world," how does that make you feel? Do you agree or disagree? Why?

2. Why do people confuse *being* rich with *feeling* rich?

3. Describe a time when you noticed that the more that you had, the more you wanted. When you feed an appetite, what happens to it? Why?

4. In the video, Andy says "wealth can become a substitute for God." Do you believe that your hope could migrate from dependency on God to dependency on money? Why or why not?

5. Read 1 Timothy 6:17–19 together as a group. Do you tend to think of Christians and the church as being generous? Why or why not?

6. How could being generous to others change people's perceptions of Christians and the church?

7. Why do we hesitate to give to others even though we have more than we need?

MOVING FORWARD

Most of us have to come to terms with the fact that we are rich. But, unfortunately, most of us don't know how to BE RICH. During this study, we will be challenged to think deeply about what it means to be rich and how to become generous people.

What can you do this week to be rich toward others? How can your group support each other to become generous people?

BETWEEN SESSIONS

1. Memorize these key verses during the coming week:

> Command those who are rich in this pres-
> ent world not to be arrogant nor to put their
> hope in wealth, which is so uncertain, but
> to put their hope in God, who richly pro-
> vides us with everything for our enjoyment.
> Command them to do good, to be rich in
> good deeds, and to be generous and willing
> to share.
>
> *(1 Timothy 6:17–18)*

2. Read the introduction and chapters 1 and 2 of this book before your small group meets for Session 2.

SESSION 2: SIDE EFFECTS

INTRODUCTION

Rich people live in denial. They won't admit they're rich. No matter how much you have, there's always someone who has more. But if you earn $37,000 a year, you are in the top 4 percent of wage earners in the world. If you earn $48,000 a year, you are in the top 1 percent of wage earners in the world. Most of us are rich. And one of the dangers of being rich is discontentment. The more you have, the more you want.

Wealth has side effects. If you're rich, you're at risk. How do we avoid the pitfalls of wealth?

VIDEO VIEWING AND NOTES

Watch the Session 2 video, "Side Effects," together as a group and note anything that impacts you.

VIDEO DISCUSSION

1. How do you define "rich"? How much money does someone have to make in order to be considered wealthy?

2. When it comes to money and finances, what are your hopes, dreams, and goals?

3. In the video, Andy asked the question, "How much money would you need to secure your future against all imaginable eventualities?" What went through your mind?

4. Which of these statements creates more anxiety in you: "There is no God" or "There is no money"? Why?

5. Read 1 Timothy 6:17 together as a group. How does this passage challenge your assumptions about wealth?

6. Why do you think that Paul commands those who are rich not to be arrogant?

7. Wealth and God will always be in competition for your heart. How can you prevent your heart from migrating from God?

MOVING FORWARD

If you're wealthy, don't be arrogant. Be grateful. Don't lean on your wealth. Lean on the One who gave you your wealth. That way, you can have peace in your heart as well as money in the bank. Make this daily declaration a part of your life: "I will not place my trust in riches, but in him who richly provides."

What is one thing you can do this week to begin to put your hope in God instead of your wealth? What can your group do to support each other to put your hope in God?

BETWEEN SESSIONS

1. Memorize this key verse for the coming week:

    > No one can serve two masters. Either you will
    > hate the one and love the other, or you will be
    > devoted to the one and despise the other. You
    > cannot serve both God and money.
    >
    > *(Matthew 6:24)*

2. Read chapters 3 and 4 of this book before your small
    group meets for Session 3.

SESSION 3: DOLLAR COST LIVING

INTRODUCTION

For many of us, our problem isn't that we're not rich; our problem is that we don't feel rich. The desire to feel wealthy causes us to place our hope in money instead of in God. But the Bible describes a different way of thinking about and using our wealth.

Talk about a time when you gave money to someone in need. How did it make you feel?

VIDEO VIEWING AND NOTES

Watch the Session 3 video, "Dollar Cost Living," together as a group and note anything that impacts you.

VIDEO DISCUSSION

1. In the video, Andy says that the key to feeling rich isn't making a lot of money but having financial margin. Does that ring true to you? Why or why not?

2. What is one thing that stands in the way of you being a percentage giver instead of a spontaneous giver? What is one thing you can do to overcome that obstacle?

3. What kinds of things could you and your church accomplish in your community if everyone became percentage givers?

4. What most excites you about giving money to help others?

5. Read 1 Timothy 6:18 together as a group. What are ways that we can be rich in good deeds when our daily schedules are so filled with activity?

6. In the video, Andy says that Paul's point to Timothy is that rich people should give larger sums and higher percentages. Do you agree? Why or why not?

7. How do you think the early Christians practiced generosity and a willingness to share? (See Acts 2:42–47.)

MOVING FORWARD

To keep your hope from migrating, decide ahead of time to do more and give more. If God has blessed you with more than you need, it is so that you can share your abundance with those in need. Do and give systematically. Can you imagine what would happen if everyone did that?

What is one step you can take this week toward becoming a percentage giver rather than a spontaneous giver? What can your group do to support each other to be rich in good deeds and more generous?

BETWEEN SESSIONS

1. Memorize this key verse for the coming week:

   > Command them to do good, to be rich in
   > good deeds, and to be generous and willing
   > to share.
   >
   > *(1 Timothy 6:18)*

2. Read chapters 5 and 6 of this book before your small
   group meets for Session 4.

SESSION 4: DIVERSIFY

INTRODUCTION

We're all tempted to place our faith in money. We're tempted to believe that if we make enough, we'll be able to control our circumstances and create a better life for ourselves. The problem with that view is that the more we place our faith in the money, the more it controls us. Scripture challenges us to look at our money differently because our lives are better when we place our trust in the One who richly provides. Viewing wealth through the lens of eternity loosens our grip on it and its grip on us.

How has your view toward wealth changed over the course of reading *How to Be Rich* and watching the videos during your small group?

VIDEO VIEWING AND NOTES

Watch the Session 4 video, "Diversify," together as a group and note anything that impacts you.

VIDEO DISCUSSION

1. In the video, Andy says that we don't get credit for what we leave but for what we give. What's your response to that idea?

2. What are ways we can loosen the grip of desiring more wealth in our lives in light of eternity?

3. What steps can we all take to help us move from being 3P Givers to becoming 3S Givers?

4. Read Luke 12:13–21 together as a group. In the parable, Jesus draws a connection between being rich toward those in need and being rich toward God. What do you like about this connection? How does it challenge you?

5. Read 1 Timothy 6:19 together as a group. Talk about creating "a firm foundation for the coming age" with your generosity. Does that idea resonate with you? Why or why not?

MOVING FORWARD

Do good for those who can't or won't do good for you. Don't place your hope in riches, but in the One who richly provides. Since you have more, do more and give more. **Remember, there's more to life than this life.**

What is one thing you can do this week to begin viewing wealth through the lens of eternity? What can your group do to support each other as you choose to loosen your grip on wealth?

CHANGING YOUR MIND

1. Memorize these key verses this coming week:

    Sell your possessions and give to the poor. Provide purses for yourselves that will not wear out, a treasure in heaven that will never fail, where no thief comes near and no moth destroys. For where your treasure is, there your heart will be also.

    (Luke 12:33–34)

2. Read chapter 7 and the conclusion of this book and reflect on how you can become a person who desires *"to do good, to be rich in good deeds, and to be generous and willing to share."*

Other Books by Andy Stanley

Creating Community
(with Bill Willits)

Communicating for a Change
(with Lane Jones)

Deep and Wide

Making Vision Stick

The Seven Checkpoints
(with Stuart Hall and Louie Giglio)

Seven Practices of Effective Ministry
(with Lane Jones and Reggie Joiner)

Deep and Wide

Creating Churches Unchurched People Love to Attend

Andy Stanley

With candor and transparency, pastor Andy Stanley explains how one of America's largest churches began with a high-profile divorce and a church split.

But that's just the beginning ...

Deep and Wide provides church leaders with an in-depth look into North Point Community Church and its strategy for creating churches unchurched people love to attend. Andy writes, "Our goal is to create weekend experiences so compelling and helpful that even the most skeptical individuals in our community would walk away with every intention of returning the following week ... with a friend!"

Andy explains his strategy for preaching and programming to "dual audiences": mature believers and cynical unbelievers. He argues that preaching to dual audiences doesn't require communicators to "dumb down" the content. According to Stanley, it's all in the approach.

> "Deep and Wide *pulls back the curtain for all of us to see what is required behind the scenes to build a prevailing church; I was both challenged and inspired by this book.*"
>
> –Bill Hybels, author of *Just Walk Across the Room*

How to Be Rich: A DVD Study

It's Not What You Have. It's What You Do With What You Have.

Andy Stanley

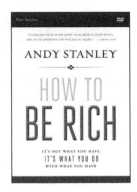

Ever stood in front of a closet full of clothes trying to find something to wear?
Ever traded in a perfectly good car for another...car?
Ever killed some time talking on your cell phone while standing in line to get a newer version of the same phone?

According to author and pastor Andy Stanley, if you answered "yes" to any of those questions, you might be rich.

But you might think, rich is the other guy. Rich is that other family. Rich is having more than you currently have. If that's the case, you can be rich and not know it. You can be rich and not feel it. You can be rich and not act like it. And that is a problem.

In this four-session small group study, Andy Stanley encourages us to consider that we may be richer than we think, and challenges us to consider that we may not be very good at it.

It's one thing to Be Rich.

Andy wants to help us all be GOOD at it!

Sessions include:

1. Congratulations
2. Side Effects
3. Dollar Cost Living
4. Diversify

How to Be Rich Church Campaign Kit

Andy Stanley

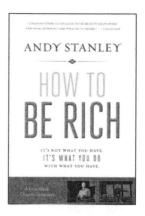

This four-week preaching series and small group study exploring 1 Timothy 6:18 is a tool that will force conversation and reflection around the topic of what to do with what we have. Jesus could not have been any clearer. It's not what you have that matters. It's what you do with what you have that will count for you or against you in the kingdom of heaven.

This campaign kit includes everything needed for a four-week church campaign:

- Starter Guide
- *How to Be Rich* softcover book
- *How to Be Rich: A DVD Study*
- Church campaign resource DVD with sermon resources, promotional resources, and campaign implementation guide

Available in stores and online!

Share Your Thoughts

With the Author: Your comments will be forwarded to the author when you send them to *zauthor@zondervan.com*.

With Zondervan: Submit your review of this book by writing to *zreview@zondervan.com*.

Free Online Resources at
www.zondervan.com

Daily Bible Verses and Devotions: Enrich your life with daily Bible verses or devotions that help you start every morning focused on God. Visit www.zondervan.com/newsletters.

Free Email Publications: Sign up for newsletters on Christian living, academic resources, church ministry, fiction, children's resources, and more. Visit www.zondervan.com/newsletters.

Zondervan Bible Search: Find and compare Bible passages in a variety of translations at www.zondervanbiblesearch.com.

Other Benefits: Register to receive online benefits like coupons and special offers, or to participate in research.